S.   Hrg.   114–187

EPA'S GOLD KING MINE DISASTER: EXAMINING THE HARMFUL IMPACTS TO INDIAN COUNTRY

HEARING

BEFORE THE

COMMITTEE ON INDIAN AFFAIRS UNITED STATES SENATE

ONE HUNDRED FOURTEENTH CONGRESS

FIRST SESSION

SEPTEMBER 16, 2015

Printed for the use of the Committee on Indian Affairs

U.S. GOVERNMENT PUBLISHING OFFICE

98–848 PDF   WASHINGTON : 2016

For sale by the Superintendent of Documents, U.S. Government Publishing Office
Internet: bookstore.gpo.gov   Phone: toll free (866) 512–1800; DC area (202) 512–1800
Fax: (202) 512–2104   Mail: Stop IDCC, Washington, DC 20402–0001

CONTENTS

EPA'S GOLD KING MINE DISASTER: EXAMINING THE HARMFUL IMPACTS TO INDIAN COUNTRY

WEDNESDAY, SEPTEMBER 16, 2015

U.S. SENATE,
COMMITTEE ON INDIAN AFFAIRS,
Washington, DC.

The Committee met, pursuant to notice, at 2:15 p.m. in room 628, Dirksen Senate Office Building, Hon. John Barrasso, Chairman of the Committee, presiding.

OPENING STATEMENT OF HON. JOHN BARRASSO, U.S. SENATOR FROM WYOMING

The CHAIRMAN. Good afternoon. I call this hearing to order.

Today we will examine the short and long-term impacts to tribal communities from the tragic spill of 3 million gallons of toxic wastewater from the Gold King Mine by Environmental Protection Agency personnel and their contractors. This toxic wastewater was first unleashed into the Cement Creek, a tributary of the Animas River, in Colorado and then flowed downstream to the San Juan River. The reach and repercussions of the August 5th disaster are substantial.

This disaster is commanding attention from no less than four congressional committees in both the House and the Senate. Just this morning, the Senate Environment and Public Works Committee, on which I also serve, held an oversight hearing on the matter.

This Committee hearing will focus on how the EPA's actions have impacted the tribal communities residing in the path of this toxic plume unleashed by the EPA. Two of those tribes, the Navajo Nation and the Southern Ute Indian Tribe, are represented here today.

The 3 million gallons of high concentrations of metals, including cadmium and lead, plus other substances such as arsenic, were released into the waterways crossing these tribal lands. The chemicals in this spill turned the creeks and rivers into rusty, contaminated sludge. Here is some of the water taken from that. There is no question that the EPA bears this responsibility.

Almost a month after the spill, we were told the waterways affected have now returned to their normal color and that conditions have returned to pre-spill levels. This does not excuse the EPA's negligence or the environmental impact to tribal communities.

Whether a private company or a Federal agency itself carelessly blew out a mining wall and unleashed 3 million gallons of toxic materials into these waterways, both should be held accountable to the communities they negatively impacted.

In the immediate aftermath of the spill, we know that at least two tribal communities were, and are still, severely impacted. Both the Southern Ute Indian Tribe and the Navajo Nation were forced to issue state of emergency declarations in response to the spill. Ranchers and farmers on the Navajo Nation suddenly could not use the river water. Livestock could not drink the water. Irrigation and canals went dry, as the pictures indicate.

Navajo President Russell Begaye stated in one press account that farmers and ranchers on the reservation have essentially "written off this year's crops." These losses are occurring in a tribal community where unemployment now stands at roughly 42 percent.

Many questions arise from this tragic, preventable spill that has hurt the peace of mind and violated the trust of these tribal communities. Why wasn't the EPA prepared to protect tribal communities in case such a blowout occurred? Once the spill happened, how did the EPA respond to address the crisis occurring within the affected tribal communities?

Several troubling conclusions are already coming to light. The first and most obvious is that a spill of this size and magnitude should never be caused by an agency whose sole mission is to protect the environment. Moreover, the EPA was not prepared to respond to the spill. The poor treatment the tribes received by the EPA as the crisis played out is simply unconscionable.

Dr. Mathy Stanislaus, the EPA official in charge of addressing the spill, stated before the House Science Committee last week, "We believe we have been as transparent as we possibly could." He also said. "I think we have been very transparent." As the tribes will testify today, they completely disagree with the EPA's rosy assessment of their actions. They do not believe they were adequately notified after the incident or consulted sufficiently with regard to remediation activities.

In testimony before the House Science Committee hearing held last week, Dr. Donald Benn of the Navajo Nation stated that the EPA "downplayed the magnitude" of the spill. The tribes also do not believe that the EPA was doing sufficient water testing. Of the testing that was conducted, the tribes indicated that the EPA was not providing them with the water quality test data and sediment test data that they requested.

Dr. Benn further testified that there is now a "culture of distrust" between the tribe and the EPA. The EPA took a series of actions that made the agency appear insensitive to the needs of the tribes. For example, the Navajo Nation, at one point, confiscated and asked residents not to use EPA-issued water tanks. There are pictures of the water tanks.

Navajo Nation officials believe the tanks were once used for oil and the Nation believed at the time that the water inside the tanks was unsafe for any use. It was a completely unacceptable response by a Federal agency to a community whose water that agency had just contaminated.

In addition, EPA officials attempted to have Navajo Nation and Southern Ute tribal members sign a form that appeared to waive his or her right to claim future damages from this spill. The question is, why did the EPA officials do this? The tribal members would have had to calculate their short and long term monetary damages without even knowing the full extent of the costs to them and what the costs would be to them and their livelihoods. This is unacceptable during a crisis when people's farms, ranches and businesses are under threat and the magnitude of the problem is still unknown.

A major question that remains is how the EPA and which individuals will be held accountable for the spill and its aftermath. The EPA's own documents and internal employee e-mails have revealed the agency officials knew about the dangers of a potential blowout at the mine.

For example, the EPA released one document to several media organizations in August stating that back in June 2014, the EPA knew ''Conditions may exist that could result in a blowout of the blockages and cause a release of large volumes of contaminated mine waters and sediment from inside the mine, which contain concentrated heavy metals.''

Let us be clear. This accident was preventable and individuals should be held accountable. The actions of this agency and agency personnel in triggering or contributing to the spill and in dealing with its aftermath in Indian Country are a case study of agency incompetence and an agency incapable of meeting its sole mission.

Their actions demonstrate why the EPA cannot be trusted to take on the array of regulatory overreaches that they have proposed. It is also a case study in how this agency disregards the needs of tribes during a crisis. These shortcomings are troubling and will be the subject of scrutiny today.

Before we receive testimony from our witnesses, I would like to ask Vice Chairman Tester if he has an opening statement?

STATEMENT OF HON. JON TESTER, U.S. SENATOR FROM MONTANA

Senator TESTER. I do.

Thank you, Mr. Chairman, for holding the hearing today to discuss the harmful impacts of the recent spill at the Gold King Mine into the Animas and San Juan Rivers and the impacts on the downstream Native communities.

I understand the Navajo Nation and the Southern Ute Tribes utilize these watersheds for irrigation, ranching and in some places, for drinking water. Any time disaster threatens a water source, it is cause for great concern, even more when it appears the Federal agency whose role it is to protect the environment has had a hand in causing the incident.

Clean water is such an important resource, one that is becoming scarcer and scarcer by the day across the West. The Federal Government, along with tribal and local partners, must ensure that these resources are protected and remain available for current and future generations.

The hearing today is entitled EPA's Gold King Mine Disaster. While I agree we must hold the government offices accountable, the

EPA alone is not responsible for this disaster. For decades, we have allowed mining companies to strip the lands of valuable resources with no plans to reclaim the landscape. Yet, we act surprised and get angry when predictable outcomes like this one occur.

The Gold King Mine, and many other like it, will continue to have long-lasting impacts to the health and well-being of nearby communities. We must find a way to address the problem now and into the future, as I am certain this will not be the last time we have to have hearings like this one in the Senate.

Now, Administrator McCarthy, your agency messed up. I do not know if it was a lack of oversight over contractors, a lack of funding or what it was. However, what happened at Gold King Mine is unacceptable. I am not sure what was worse, the spill itself or how the agency responded to it and worked with its tribal partners.

We all know it was a bad spill, we also know the mine was already leaking and will continue to leak. Our job is to make sure it is contained to allow water at clean enough levels.

You will hear from tribal leaders the impact the spill has had on their communities and local economies. Since the spill, when the agency had the opportunity to respond and take leadership in the situation with local tribes as stakeholders, I do not believe the agency stepped up to the plate like it could have.

A month later, I can tell you the tribes are still dissatisfied not just by the initial response, but the lack of ongoing commitment to help these communities. While the effects of the spill will be mitigated, distrust of the government that persists in tribal communities certainly was not improved by the EPA.

We have heard that of all the agencies that have stepped forward to address this problem, the BIA has been the most helpful. I can tell you that is not something we hear a lot of in this Committee but it is a testament to the Bureau of Indian Affairs in that it knows how to work with tribes and those relationships. That kind of knowledge would have been great for the EPA to lean on.

I encourage you to do that. There is still some time to work with tribes and other Federal partners to address the impacts of this spill.

I imagine my colleagues will take this opportunity to justify funding of the EPA. Unfortunately, that is the opposite of what needs to be done. After decades of mining activity across the Country, we need the EPA to address these issues. We need the EPA out there looking at mines to determine how to reclaim and prevent long term spills and the impacts to the environment. They are probably better at it if their funding streams were not constantly under threat.

We also need to ensure that tribes have the resources they need to protect their lands for future generations. While this is not their best example, to be sure, these are the experts who, when they team up with local and tribal communities, will continue to make sure communities are safe for people to live long and healthy lives.

I want to thank Administrator McCarthy for being here today and addressing the Committee. Thank you, President Begaye and Council Member Olguin, for coming all this way to address the impacts to your communities.

I look forward to this hearing and the testimony of the participants.

The CHAIRMAN. Thank you, Senator Tester.

Do any other members have opening statements? Senator McCain.

STATEMENT OF HON. JOHN McCAIN,
U.S. SENATOR FROM ARIZONA

Senator McCAIN. Mr. Chairman, thank you.

I think you have pretty well covered the issue. I would just like to point out that in August, I was with Arizona Governor Doug Ducey. We met with Navajo Nation President Russell Begaye and Navajo Council Speaker LoRenzo Bates in Window Rock, Arizona.

I can assure my colleagues that the Navajo are suffering deeply and dearly because of this spill. An estimated 1,500 farms on the Navajo Nation have been impacted by the 3 million gallon release of wastewater caused by EPA contractors. An acidic plume of mercury, arsenic and other metals worked its way down the Animas River in Colorado and into the San Juan River near Farmington, New Mexico.

Nobody knows for certain yet the total damage to crops, soil, livestock, wildlife and irrigation, and drinking water supplies, critical sources of food for the Navajo people and which also serve as economic and cultural centers.

Mr. Chairman, Doug Holtz-Eakin, a well known economist to many of us, will testify later on. In his testimony, he says, ''There is no direct precedent to the toxic Animas River spill in Colorado. Past EPA estimates indicate the spill could cost between $338 million and $27.7 billion.''

He goes on to say, ''The transparency within the Environmental Protection Agency remains elusive. The Gold King case shows inaction, poor planning and misleading statements by top officials. Prevention, planning and mitigation were not adequately executed.''

Mr. Chairman, I could talk a lot more about the impact this has had on the Southern Ute Tribe and the Ute Mountain Tribe but this is a very serious, serious problem. So far as I know, no one yet has been held responsible. To me, that is disgraceful, 43 days after this occurrence took place.

Thank you, Mr. Chairman.

The CHAIRMAN. Thank you, Senator McCain.

Senator Udall?

STATEMENT OF HON. TOM UDALL,
U.S. SENATOR FROM NEW MEXICO

Senator UDALL. Thank you very much, Chairman Barrasso and Vice Chairman Tester for focusing on this very, very important issue to the West and to the rest of the Nation.

In the West, our rivers are our lifelines. This is especially true for the Navajo Nation, which depends on limited surface water resources. The San Juan River is crucial and brings water for drinking, irrigation, recreation and has great cultural and religious significance to the Navajo people.

The Federal Government must own up to this tragedy. I am encouraged that we have the Administrator with us and she has taken responsibility for this accident. Those on the Navajo Nation and others affected by this spill must be compensated. I will be introducing legislation on that front with Senator Heinrich.

The Navajo Nation has been on the receiving end of disasters like this brought on by the Federal Government and others for far too long. Mistakes have been made. We need to do everything in our power to make sure they are not made again.

I recently visited the area to speak with President Begaye, from whom we will hear on the second panel, the newly inaugurated President of the Navajo Nation; Speaker LoRenzo Bates; Attorney General Branch; Gilbert Harrison; and others like Mr. Chili Yazzi of Shiprock who I see here today.

I heard their concerns, I saw the terrible impact the spill was having and I saw firsthand that farming for Navajo people is not only critically important to food production but it also impacts the traditional teachings of young people who are finding their identity through agriculture. It is easy for Washington to expect things to return to normal in due time, but it is clear this disaster will continue to affect the Navajo people for a very long time.

How did this happen? How did we get to this point? Sad to say, the Gold King abandoned mine is only one of several abandoned mines which are leaching pollutants into the Animas River. There are thousands, by some estimates, on a nationwide basis from 160,000 to 500,000 of these abandoned mines which are hurting and threatening waterways throughout the Rocky Mountain Range and the rest of the Country.

When we talk about public lands in the West, this is the legacy of the 1872 mining law, an ancient law which encouraged exploration for hard rock minerals but did nothing to compensate the public for the extraction of valuable minerals.

On top of that, it did nothing to require mines to clean up after they finished. That is the legacy of what we are seeing here today. As a result there are thousands of abandoned mines on public land, contaminated land, polluted streams and the taxpayers are having to pay for the cleanup.

I believe in the principle of polluter pays. Other, more recent laws have enshrined this principle, polluter pays, but we are stuck with the 1872 mining law which requires none of this. That is what the big mining companies are doing, refusing reform and refusing to pay.

Some of the people who have looked at this area say the 1872 mining law and its supervision of mining is some of the most lax public oversight of any industry. We cannot continue that way.

I would hearken back to before I got into the House. Some of the Senators on this panel were probably there in the House or the Senate. Newt Gingrich saw the ripping off of the taxpayers and passed a bipartisan bill through the House of Representatives reforming the 1872 mining law. It had a 300 vote margin.

This can be done if we put our heads together and work with each other. I am very encouraged that we have a bipartisan effort here on the Committee. I look forward to working with our Colorado Senators who were impacted and then the flow came into New Mexico.

Thank you very much, Mr. Chairman, again for focusing on this.

The CHAIRMAN. Thank you, Senator Udall.

We will hear from both of the Colorado Senators starting with Senator Gardner.

STATEMENT OF HON. CORY GARDNER, U.S. SENATOR FROM COLORADO

Senator GARDNER. Thank you, Mr. Chairman. Thank you for holding this hearing today.

Thank you to Vice Chairman Tester for participating and making this happen today as well.

Administrator McCarthy, thank you for being here.

I want to reiterate the comments made by my colleague from New Mexico about the impacts of water on our western States.

If you go into the capitol of Colorado in the rotunda, there is a mural painted on the wall. The beginning of the mural states something like this, ''Here is a land where history is written in water.'' Those words are two or three stories below one of the most iconic legacies of mining in Colorado. That is Colorado's golden dome of our State capitol.

This morning we talked about the impact it has had. Mike Olguin, a tribal council member from the Southern Ute Tribe, is here today to talk about the impact the spill had on the Southern Ute Tribe. We talked about the response of the EPA to the spill.

We have questions that have to be answered. I hope not only your testimony this morning and your testimony this afternoon but the ongoing investigations will provide greater insight into what exactly happened.

I will share with you what I shared this morning. In the days and hours after the spill occurred, response came from the State of Colorado. We learned about the EPA spill not from the EPA but from the Durango Herald.

In our attempts to contact you and the office, we were told that you were unavailable. After pushing back, we were advised we could speak to the regional director and that phone call occurred several hours after that. I think you and I spoke sometime as late as August 11 for the first time.

In the days after this event occurred, the community of Durango, the community of southwestern Colorado, and the tribes were left with a lot of questions. In fact, four days after the spill occurred, Senator Bennet and I were at a community meeting in Durango where the results of testing and water samples were displayed on a projector in front of the community talking about the levels of contaminants in the water.

Yet, there was no explanation at all whatsoever was given as to what those levels meant. Was it unhealthy? Was it healthy? Was it dangerous? Was it not dangerous? We were told at that conference call that we would be provided with an analysis of those numbers.

Later on in the day when another briefing occurred, there was no analysis. Days went by before there were any answers provided. Long after the flash of the television cameras go away in southwestern Colorado, we will be dealing with this and the questions.

We have to find answers to things like where was the EPA during the initial notification and closure of the river? Did the agency follow the national contingency plan for notification and implementation of the disaster? Was there anyone within the EPA crisis management team with experience for a spill of this nature dispatched to the area or made aware of the spill immediately? These are just a few of the questions we will discuss.

As we will hear in Councilmember Olguin's testimony, in the first few days following the spill, it was largely State, local and tribal officials responding. Not until August 10th did the EPA establish a unified command center in Durango. Along with the confusion over EPA's lack of notification, frustration began regarding the need for timely release of simple, straightforward interpretation of water quality monitoring data from the EPA.

The long term questions remain. What happens when you disturb the river? In conversations from Silverton to Durango, hotel rooms were canceled and bookings were canceled.

In fact, even the president of the Ft. Lewis College talked about the fact that parents from around the Country had called their school to make sure it was okay for their child to go back to school. Yet, days later, we still did not have answers.

I appreciate the hearing, I appreciate the answers as we work on water treatment and the need for a water treatment facility; as we work on the need, not just to talk about Good Samaritan legislation, not just to introduce Good Samaritan legislation, but to actually pass it in a bipartisan fashion.

I commend the Senators from New Mexico and my colleague, Senator Bennet from Colorado, on the need to not just talk about it and introduce it, but to actually pass it to law and on the President's desk, that we can begin to do good to address the 23,000 mines in Colorado alone.

I thank you for your time and the opportunity to speak today.

The CHAIRMAN. Thank you, Senator Gardner.

Senator BENNET.

STATEMENT OF HON. MICHAEL F. BENNET, U.S. SENATOR FROM COLORADO

Senator BENNET. Thank you, Mr. Chairman. Thank you and Senator Tester for including my colleague from Colorado and myself. It is a privilege to be here with my colleague from New Mexico as well. I wish it were under other circumstances but it is not.

The blowout at the Gold King Mine was a disaster that affected many communities in Colorado and New Mexico. Although the EPA was working to try to evaluate how to clean up the mine, there is no denying that the EPA caused this spill. That is entirely unacceptable.

It is also clear, as my colleagues from Colorado and New Mexico said, the agency was slow to communicate with local governments, did not obtain water quality results or bring water to farmers who needed it much more quickly than it was delivered.

Senator Gardner and I traveled together to Durango four days after the blowout, the river was still bright orange and closed to the public. As said here today about New Mexico and Colorado, the Animas River really is the lifeblood of southwestern Colorado and Durango.

Rafting companies have lost business, farmers could not water crops and moms are still keeping their kids out of the river. These families deserve to have the full attention and dedicated resources of the Administration committed to this cleanup.

In the week after the spill, we spoke with Administrator McCarthy and wrote to the EPA and the President. We appreciate that the Administrator listened to our call and came to Colorado to view the area and address the community.

Following a crisis like this, it is important to make sure we hold people and agencies accountable for any egregious mistakes or negligence committed in the days and hours after the spill. As our communities recover, it is also critical, as my colleagues from New Mexico and Colorado said, we need to look at the bigger picture. Let us identify exactly what went wrong and make sure it does not happen again.

We also need to put this in context. The blowout released 3 million gallons of acid mud drainage. The same amount of polluted water was already being released from the Gold King Mine around every week. The four mines near it release more than 300 million gallons of acid mine drainage into the river every year.

This has been going on for more than 130 years. In 1902, the water quality was so bad that Durango permanently switched to the Florida River for its main drinking supply. That decision by our forbearers protected the town's drinking water from the most recent disaster.

There are more than 23,000 abandoned mines in Colorado, including 400 in the San Juan Mountains alone. We need solutions to address the acid mine drainage coming from all these old abandoned mines.

We need to pass Good Samaritan legislation, as Senator Gardner said. I think we also need to address the 1872 Mining Act.

In the aftermath of the spill, the Southern Ute Tribe acted quickly to notify other tribes and local governments, began water sampling of its own and provided water for livestock. The tribal leadership closely collaborated with local governments, sister tribes, the EPA and the State.

In this crisis, they demonstrated their expertise, their professionalism and their leadership. Mr. Mike Olguin was an integral part of that effort. We are lucky that he will be on the second panel today. He has served the tribe for 37 years and has a vast source of knowledge for all of us.

I just wanted to come to this hearing to be able to say we are delighted he is able to join the Senate today and share his experiences during this disaster.

Thank you again, Mr. Chairman, for allowing me this time.

The CHAIRMAN. Thank you very much, Senator Bennet. Senator Heinrich.

STATEMENT OF HON. MARTIN HEINRICH, U.S. SENATOR FROM NEW MEXICO

Senator HEINRICH. Thank you, Chairman Barrasso.

I want to thank you and the Ranking Member for holding what I think is a very important hearing today. I want to thank you for allowing me to join you on the dais for this hearing.

I also want to recognize the incredible work of Senators Gardner and Bennet and my senior Senator, Tom Udall, as well as Congressman Ben Ray Lujan, in focusing on this issue on a number of policy fronts.

You all heard about the plume last month. It was something to see. It is not normal to look at a trout stream and see it look like the color of Tang. That is exactly what we all saw.

I want to share the fact that basically I share the anger and frustration over this incident. When I toured the affected area following the spill and had a chance to visit with President Begaye of the Navajo Nation, who I am glad we will hear from this afternoon, as he can attest, the Navajo Nation did not receive timely notification from the EPA that the spill had occurred. That was something I think was true of a number of other government entities and agencies as well.

Because water intake from the San Juan River had to cease, water had to be delivered to homes, for agriculture and livestock purposes. Unfortunately, problems related to water delivery caused further concern to farmers and ranchers. Mr. Gilbert Harrison, a fellow New Mexican, is here today to tell us more specifically how the spill affected him and his fellow farmers and ranchers.

I demanded that the EPA act with urgency to protect our health and safety and to repair the damage inflicted on this watershed. That should be our first line of business in this.

Last month's spill was not the first major spill to affect the Navajo Nation. If we know our history, in 1979, a breached dam at the uranium mill tailings pond disposal pond near Church Rock actually sent more than 1,000 tons of solid radioactive waste and 93 million gallons of acid liquid waste into the Rio Puerco.

We cannot let history repeat itself over and over and over again. We must take action to address the hundreds of thousands of other similarly contaminated mines to the Gold King that litter the West today that are leaking toxins into our watersheds.

I shared a couple of maps this morning at the Environment and Public Works hearing. If you look at northern New Mexico and southwest Colorado, it is literally covered with thousands of unreclaimed or abandoned mines.

That means that developing a comprehensive approach to mine reform, which should include the establishment of a hard rock reclamation fund funded by a fair royalty on public minerals, as well as Good Samaritan authority to allow third parties to clean up mines that they had no role in creating, and I would say a comprehensive survey of abandoned mines and a plan to clean them up should all be on our menu.

For far too long, Indian Country has been left to fend for itself in dealing with the impacts of mining. In my State, too many Native communities, including many on the Navajo Nation, live among abandoned uranium mining and milling sites that still contaminate their water, air and food today.

Hard rock mines provided the raw materials to build this Country. During the Cold War, uranium from New Mexico was transformed into nuclear weapons to defend our Nation. We owe it to these communities to clean up these sites once and for all. We should not wait for disasters like this one to strike again.

Thank you again for holding this hearing. I look forward to hearing from the witnesses today.

The CHAIRMAN. Thank you, Senator Heinrich, for joining us today.

We have two panels. On the first panel, we will hear from Administrator McCarthy. Administrator McCarthy, thank you for being here. We will respect your timeline. I know you need to leave at 3:30 p.m., so please proceed.

STATEMENT OF HON. GINA McCARTHY, ADMINISTRATOR, U.S. ENVIRONMENTAL PROTECTION AGENCY

Ms. McCARTHY. Good afternoon Chairman Barrasso, Vice Chairman Tester and members of the Committee.

I am Gina McCarthy, Administrator for the U.S. Environmental Protection Agency. I want to thank you for the opportunity to appear today to discuss the August 5 Gold King Mine release and subsequent EPA response.

This was a tragic and unfortunate incident, and the EPA has taken responsibility to ensure that it is cleaned up appropriately. The EPA's core mission, as we have noted, is to ensure a clean environment and protect public health. We are dedicated to continuing to do our job to protect the environment and to hold ourselves accountable at to the same high standard we demand from others.

The EPA was at the Gold King Mine on August 5th conducting an investigation to assess mine conditions and ongoing water discharges, dewater the mine pool, and assess the feasibility of further mine remediation. While excavating above a mine opening, the lower portion of the bedrock crumbled and approximately 3 million gallons of pressurized water discharged from the mine into Cement Creek, a tributary of the Animas River.

EPA and Colorado officials informed downstream EPA and Colorado officials informed downstream jurisdictions in Colorado within hours of the release before the plume reached drinking water intakes and irrigation diversions, and notifications to other downstream jurisdictions continued the following day, allowing for those intakes to be closed prior to the plume's arrival.

In the aftermath of the release, we initiated an internal review of the incident and released an Internal Review Summary Report on August, 26, which includes an assessment of the events and potential factors contributing to the Gold King Mine incident. The report provides observations, conclusions, and recommendations that regions really must consider when conducting ongoing and planned site assessments, investigations, and construction or removal projects at similar types of sites across the Country. The EPA will implement all the recommendations from the report and has shared its findings with external reviewers.

In addition to the internal review, the U.S. Department of the Interior is leading an independent assessment of the factors that led to the Gold King Mine incident. The goal of DOI's independent review is to provide the EPA with an analysis of the incident that took place at Gold King Mine, including the contributing causes. Both internal and external reviews will help inform the EPA for ongoing and planned site assessments, investigations, and construction or removal projects.

One of our foremost priorities is to keep the public informed about the impacts from the Gold King Mine release and our response activities. The EPA has closely coordinated with our Federal partners and with officials in Colorado, New Mexico, Utah, the Southern Ute and Ute Mountain Ute tribes and the Navajo Nation to keep them apprised of water and sediment sampling results, which are routinely posted on our website. These results indicate that water and sediment have returned to pre-event conditions and supported local and State decision-makers as they made the decision to lift water restrictions along the Animas and San Juan Rivers.

Finally, I want to clarify that the EPA was working with the State of Colorado to take action at the Gold King Mine to address both the potential for a catastrophic release and the ongoing adverse water quality impacts caused by the significant mine discharges into the Upper Animas Watershed.

Based upon 2009–2014 flow data, approximately 330 million gallons of contaminated water was being discharged from mines in the watershed each year to Cement Creek and the Animas River, 100 times more than the estimated release from the Gold King Mine on August 5th. The EPA was and continues to work with the State of Colorado and the Animas River Stakeholder Group to address these significant discharges from mines in the Upper Animas Watershed that are impacting these waterways.

I think it is important to note that all across the Country, our Superfund program has successfully cleaned up more than 1,150 hazardous waste sites and successfully responded to or provided oversight for thousands of removal actions to protect human health and the environment. That reflects our longstanding commitment to protect human health and the environment. All of the affected residents of Colorado and New Mexico and the tribes can be assured that the EPA has and will continue to take responsibility to help ensure that the Gold King Mine release is cleaned up.

Thank you, Mr. Chairman. That concludes my statement. I will be happy to answer any questions that you or the Committee members may have.

[The prepared statement of Ms. McCarthy follows:]

PREPARED STATEMENT OF HON. GINA MCCARTHY, ADMINISTRATOR, U.S. ENVIRONMENTAL PROTECTION AGENCY

Good afternoon Chairman Barrasso, Vice Chairman Tester and Members of the Committee. I am Gina McCarthy, Administrator for the U.S. Environmental Protection Agency. Thank you for the opportunity to appear today to discuss the August 5 Gold King Mine release and subsequent EPA response.

This was a tragic and unfortunate incident, and the EPA has taken responsibility to ensure that it is cleaned up appropriately. The EPA's core mission is to ensure a clean environment and protect public health, and we are dedicated to continuing to do our job to protect the environment and to hold ourselves to the same high standard we demand from others.

The EPA was at the Gold King Mine on August 5 conducting an investigation to assess mine conditions and ongoing water discharges, dewater the mine pool, and assess the feasibility of further mine remediation. While excavating above a mine opening, the lower portion of the bedrock crumbled and approximately three million gallons of pressurized water discharged from the mine into Cement Creek, a tributary of the Animas River. EPA and Colorado officials informed downstream jurisdictions in Colorado within hours of the release before the plume reached drinking water intakes and irrigation diversions, and notifications to other downstream jurisdictions continued the following day, allowing for those intakes to be closed prior to the plume's arrival.

In the aftermath of the release, we initiated an internal review of the incident and released an Internal Review Summary Report on August, 26, which includes an assessment of the events and potential factors contributing to the Gold King Mine incident. The report provides observations, conclusions, and recommendations that regions should consider applying when conducting ongoing and planned site assessments, investigations, and construction or removal projects at similar types of sites across the country. The EPA will implement all the recommendations from the report and has shared its findings with external reviewers.

In addition to the internal review, the U.S. Department of the Interior is leading an independent assessment of the factors that led to the Gold King Mine incident. The goal of DOI's independent review is to provide the EPA with an analysis of the incident that took place at Gold King Mine, including the contributing causes. Both internal and external reviews will help inform the EPA for ongoing and planned site assessments, investigations, and construction or removal projects.

One of our foremost priorities is to keep the public informed about the impacts from the Gold King Mine release and our response activities. The EPA has closely coordinated with our federal partners and with officials in Colorado, New Mexico, Utah, the Southern Ute and Ute Mountain Ute tribes and the Navajo Nation to keep them apprised of water and sediment sampling results, which are routinely posted on our website. These results indicate that water and sediment have returned to pre-event conditions and supported local and state decision-makers as they made the decision to lift water restrictions along the Animas and San Juan Rivers on August 14 and August 15.

Finally, I want to clarify that the EPA was working with the state of Colorado to take action at the Gold King Mine to address both the potential for a catastrophic release and the ongoing adverse water quality impacts caused by the significant mine discharges into the Upper Animas Watershed.

Based upon 2009–2014 flow data, approximately 330 million gallons of contaminated water was being discharged from mines in the Watershed each year to Cement Creek and the Animas River—100 times more than the estimated release from the Gold King Mine on August 5.

The EPA was and continues to work with the State of Colorado and the Animas River Stakeholder Group to address these significant discharges from mines in the Upper Animas Watershed that are impacting these waterways.

I think it is important to note, that all across the country, our Superfund program has successfully cleaned up more than 1,150 hazardous waste sites and successfully responded to or provided oversight for thousands of removal actions to protect human health and the environment. That reflects our long-standing commitment to protect human health and the environment that we will continue to pursue and continue to support the Administration's request for an Abandoned Mine Lands fee to help cover the costs of cleanups at these sites.

All of the affected residents of Colorado and New Mexico and members of the Southern Ute, Ute Mountain Ute, and Navajo Nation Tribes can be assured that the EPA has and will continue to take responsibility to help ensure that the Gold King Mine release is cleaned up.

Thank you Mr. Chairman that concludes my statement. I will be happy to answer any questions that you or the Committee members may have.

The CHAIRMAN. Thank you. I will begin.

On August 24, 2015, an EPA internal review of the blowout report made several recommendations. One recommendation was the EPA should develop guidance outlining the steps that should be taken to minimize the risk of future blowouts.

Could you tell us how far along the EPA is in identifying contingency plans in the event of future blowouts at the Gold King Mine or other mines?

Ms. McCARTHY. What I decided to do was put a hiatus on these types of actions until we had the complete information from DOI's independent review of the situation. Until that is done, anything we do would not be complete enough and would not assure me that the same situation would not arise again.

We have two responsibilities. We need to clean this up and we need to make sure it never happens again.

The CHAIRMAN. In terms of the cleanup, during the EPA briefing for Committee staff last week, the agency officials were asked why the resources like water and hay for livestock and additional environmental testing were being pulled back from the tribes.

The agency officials told the Committee staff that the resource decision was based on the Center for Disease Control's recommendation that there would be no threat of health impacts of exposure.

According to EPA's own Children Environmental Health Facts website, it says ''Currently no level of lead in the blood can be identified as safe for children. I believe, as a doctor, that we need to be concerned about that.''

The agency releases 3 million gallons of toxic pollutants, heavy metals, including lead, into waterways which cross these lands of the tribes. Can you tell this Committee and the tribes represented here today that you know there will not be any health impacts to the tribal communities and their children from this poisonous spill? At this point, the resources have been pulled back because they say everything is safe.

Ms. McCARTHY. Let me answer your question and clarify just a little bit.

Because of the quick action of President Begaye, there was no input of this water into drinking water supplies. The challenge I think we are working through with the president is to really look at how that it is returned to pre-event conditions, the quality of the water now according to EPA samples and the tribe has split sampled and taken their own, that is returned to pre-event conditions. This water was never a pristine water supply because of the discharges from the Animas.

The qualification I want to bring to this, Mr. Chairman, is I want it to be very clear that we are continuing to provide hay. The BIA and EPA have continued all along to provide water for livestock and irrigation purposes. The BIA is going to continue.

We have ongoing conversations with the tribes so I do not want anyone in this Committee to think that we are going to arbitrarily shut off the support that we owe to this tribe but we are entering a more discrete and detailed discussion about what would make the tribe basically more comfortable in terms of the uses of this water and what else we need to do not just beyond that but to address the cultural and other challenges the spill has thrust upon the Navajo.

The CHAIRMAN. Since responsibility for the spill lies with the EPA, the agency I believe has to go above and beyond the standard response to address the needs of the communities impacted, specifically the tribal communities.

Private entities that pollute are held to a very strict standard by the EPA and are routinely investigated by the EPA and the Justice Department. The question today is has anyone been fired at the EPA as a result of this spill, has anyone been disciplined, suspended, reassigned, sanctioned in any way as a result of the spill? Has anyone been held accountable for the actions that resulted in this spill?

Ms. McCarthy. If you look at what led to the actions EPA took, you would see that both EPA and the Colorado Division of Reclamation, Mining and Safety worked together to develop this work plan that was carried out.

Whether or not we took every precaution and made sound judgments is something I am awaiting from the DOI independent look as opposed to making judgment based solely on our internal review. I think everyone would agree that it is good to get independent eyes on this. If we find inaccuracies, improprieties or bad judgment, we will take action.

The Chairman. At this point, no one has been held accountable for the actions. You are awaiting the report?

Ms. McCarthy. The agency itself has been held accountable. We are responding as robustly as we can to meet those responsibilities.

The Chairman. There are at least three ongoing reviews or investigations into the spill, the first being an internal review conducted by the EPA. The second is a technical review to be conducted by the Department of Interior to which you referred.

The technical review is limited to looking at causes and recommendations for solutions, not really to investigate negligence or criminal wrong-doing by the EPA.

The third review is the one requested by Congress to the EPA's Inspector General, not by you but by Congress, to look at actual wrong-doing and negligence.

Is it safe to say without Congress, not one independent investigation of negligence by the EPA would be providing an impartial review?

Ms. McCarthy. No, sir. This accident, this spill was large enough and damaging enough to the communities around it and downstream, as well as EPA's reputation, that no matter what happened, we would be looking at this spill and taking appropriate action.

The Chairman. Thank you. Senator Udall?

Senator Udall. Thank you very much, Mr. Chairman.

Administrator McCarthy, thank you so much. I know you testified this morning extensively in your authorizing committee, the Environment and Public Works Committee. You also agreed to come here and testify.

As you and I talked, the Native American community across the Country uses this Committee as a great oversight entity. We very much appreciate having you here today.

I understand the EPA is processing claims for damages under the Federal Tort Claims Act. There are advantages to this in that the U.S. Judgment Fund does not require further appropriation to compensate people.

However, under normal circumstances, Federal agencies try to limit their tort liability. That is the natural position of any defending party in the tort claims process. I do not believe that is appropriate in this kind of situation and that is why we are introducing legislation to separately guide the compensation process with a dedicated office at EPA.

Do I have your commitment that you will work diligently with the Navajo and all other victims of this spill so that all legitimate damage claims are handled quickly and appropriately without the agency trying to avoid responsibility?

Ms. MCCARTHY. You do, Senator, yes.

Senator UDALL. Thank you very much.

I would like to get your commitment here at the hearing that EPA is dedicated to prioritizing funding and resources for long term monitoring of the river and for compensation for those impacted.

Ms. MCCARTHY. That is our responsibility. We will meet that.

Senator UDALL. Thank you.

I understand from the crisis and from other past incidents, there has not always been a tremendous amount of trust between the EPA and the Navajo Nation, although I know you have a good working relationship.

The Navajo Nation has one of the most sophisticated EPAs of any tribe in the Country and you work together. Are you will to ensure a third party verification and validation on issues that may require analysis and data?

Ms. MCCARTHY. We have already begun those conversations. You have my word that we will continue to work with the president as well as Dr. Benn. I have great respect for both the leadership of the tribe and for the technical expertise. We will work together to resolve these issues.

Senator UDALL. Thank you.

The President of the Navajo Nation has requested that EPA designate the Upper Animas District as a Superfund site. I support this and believe it should be a priority for funds and remediation.

Where does the EPA stand on this question? If it was designated on the National Priorities List, how would that translate to help for the Navajo Nation which is located south of the area?

Ms. MCCARTHY. We certainly will take that request seriously. In fact, Mathy Stanislaus, our Assistant Administrator, was actually in Colorado discussing this very issue with Durango and some of the surrounding communities.

It is extremely important. It is something we have been actually been soliciting interest in for many years because we think it is the only way you are going to get significant Federal funding to support those cleanup efforts. Short of some other congressional action, there is simply no way to pass that job off to somebody else.

Senator UDALL. My understanding is there are recent press reports where all of you at the EPA are trying to organize in the valley some treatment. You talked about the 330 million gallons and to get a treatment process where we can restore those streams.

Is that part of the Superfund or is that just under your responsibilities right now without a listing?

Ms. MCCARTHY. We are going to continue to work with the State of Colorado and all of the folks downstream to look at what we can do to address those upstream issues. Part of the challenged we created with the spill was to see through both the cleanup of the spill but also to get another level of seriousness about getting at the entire comprehensive Animas Watershed.

Right now we are developing a long range monitoring plan and to do that in concert with all of the surrounding communities who will provide input. That is one of the issues we are trying to make sure the Navajo feels comfortable weighing in on and they have the ability to have a voice in that issue. It is going to be extraordinarily important that we get that started soon.

Senator UDALL. Thank you very much, Madam Administrator, for those very forthright answers.

Thank you, Mr. Chairman.

The CHAIRMAN. Thank you, Senator Udall.

Senator McCain?

Senator McCAIN. Thank you, Administrator, for coming before the Committee today.

I understand in response to the Chairman's question, no one from the EPA or the contractor has been fired, is that right?

Ms. McCARTHY. That is correct.

Senator McCAIN. No one has been fired for taking almost two days to notify the Navajo about the disaster?

Ms. McCARTHY. I might dispute a little bit how much time was taken. The first day we did notify folks and tribes in Colorado. The second day we actually did receive notification to everybody else downstream.

Senator McCAIN. So it took two days to notify the Navajo Nation. Has anyone been fired for the Navajos complaint that notification and emergency response was not adequate?

Ms. McCARTHY. We actually did send a signal through a memo that we had to look at our notification process. I am not saying that it could not have been and should not have been quicker and more comprehensive. We worked with the State on that. We are going to update our systems.

Senator McCAIN. Your answer is no.

Has anyone been fired at EPA for complaints that the EPA did not quickly and routinely share water quality monitoring data with the tribes?

Ms. McCARTHY. We believe we have done a good job in providing transparency on that data.

Senator McCAIN. You believe that but the people who were supposed to be notified do not believe that they were quickly and routinely provided the data on water quality monitor. Nor do they agree that the notification and emergency response was adequate, nor do they agree that it should have taken two days to notify the Navajo about the disaster. In other words, you have done nothing.

Tell me something, Administrator. If a mining company caused an accident like this, may be you can submit for the record an answer of what kind of penalties, fines and enforcement action the EPA would levy. I would be interested in that.

You said in response to a question by the Chairman that the agency is responsible?

Ms. McCARTHY. Yes, sir.

Senator McCAIN. Isn't the agency composed of people, so when the agency is responsible, then people are responsible?

Ms. McCARTHY. There is no question that if we find anyone has not done their job appropriately, we will.

Senator McCAIN. Someone is responsible for the accident that happened. An accident happened. A river was polluted and people were not notified.

Ms. McCARTHY. An accident happened.

Senator McCain. We all know what happened. Why is it that you are saying you do not know that anyone was responsible? Someone has to be.

Ms. McCarthy. I am not saying that the acts of the agency did not cause the accident but accidents, by their very nature, may not have resulted from any negligence whatsoever on the part of anyone.

Senator McCain. You really believe that the spill could have been through no negligence on the part of anyone?

Ms. McCarthy. I believe that we went in there with the State of Colorado having fully vetted this work plan with mining experts from the area as well as the public. Apparently all of the experts agreed this was the next step to take.

They made a judgment that we can see in our internal review that there was not an opportunity or a high pressure situation. That judgment obviously was incorrect. Whether or not they did due diligence in coming to that conclusion is what the DOI is looking at.

Senator McCain. That is almost classic. Here we are with a disaster of incredible proportions and you do not think it is best to be determined whether somebody is responsible for a decision that caused this kind of an incredible disaster and could impact the lives of Native Americans for a long period of time.

Ms. McCarthy. Sir, I am not trying to defend anybody but we went into an extraordinarily difficult situation at the request of the State for the very reason that people were worried about a blowout.

Did we intend to be the ones to trigger that? Absolutely not. Are we going to take responsibility if we did something wrong? We will.

Senator McCain. There have been other times where things have happened where it was not intended to happen. This is really classic on your part, I must say. Someone is responsible for disrupting and harming the lives and welfare and someone should be held responsible because it happened.

Maybe there were the best of intentions, Administrator McCarty, but the fact is it happened. So far no one has been held responsible except "the agency."

I have no more questions.

The Chairman. Thank you, Senator McCain.

Senator Bennet?

Senator Bennet. Thank you, Mr. Chairman.

In your answers to Senator McCain, Madam Administrator, you talked about how the agency should have been quicker and comprehensive in your communications with the tribes and others. I fully agree with that.

How are we going to make sure, what are the protocols you are putting in place to make sure that next time we get it right instead of getting it wrong?

Ms. McCarthy. All of our regions are going to be working with the States in their notification process so that we update all the lists and test it periodically to make sure of all the intakes and structures we knew about and took care of so there would not be extensive damage.

I am not suggesting that this was not a disaster because it clearly was from everyone's perspective but the notifications did go in time for us to beat the plume before those intakes would have caused damage or brought it into drinking water supplies.

We are continuing to monitor that. We have done hundreds and hundreds of tests collaboratively with all of the States and with the tribes to make sure we are keeping on top of this.

Senator BENNET. My colleague from Colorado raised this as well. Sometimes when information is produced but not explained, that can be as bad as keeping information hidden. Working on your approach to that I think is also very, very important.

Ms. MCCARTHY. I think we have talked about that, yes.

Senator BENNET. We have asked you and the President to find resources and try to prioritize funding for a water treatment plant in the Upper Animas River. We need that funding and that water treatment plant to, in the end, solve the problem of mine drainage from the four large mines. Can you tell us where that sits at the moment?

Ms. MCCARTHY. At the moment, we are working on what the long term plan should be. We have to sit down with the State of Colorado to understand what peoples' input is right now in terms of their inclination on NPL listing as well as what kind of resources can we bring to the table to begin the work.

We have already created the treatment system but it is not where it needs to be to take care of the entire problem just to increase flow that resulted from the spill. We still have huge amounts of work to do.

Senator BENNET. My understanding is that current temporary answer is not something that is suitable for the winter months. Is that right?

Ms. MCCARTHY. I will go back and check that. I am not aware of that.

Senator BENNET. If you could, that would be good.

I hear from colleague from New Mexico on Superfund status. That obviously is a very sensitive issue in our State.

Ms. MCCARTHY. It is.

Senator BENNET. My hope is that as you work toward a decision that you will engage everyone in Colorado on this question. There are different points of view as you know. The details of this matter a great deal to the people of southwestern Colorado and our State as a whole.

Ms. MCCARTHY. I want you to know that the meeting was at the request of those communities. We will continue to explain the situation. Folks will have to work with us to understand what the best way is to approach this.

Senator BENNET. We are prepared to do that.

Thank you.

Thank you, Mr. Chairman.

The CHAIRMAN. Thank you, Senator Bennet.

Senator Gardner?

Senator GARDNER. Thank you, Mr. Chairman.

Again, thank you, Administrator McCarthy.

When was the first time after August 5th that you spoke with Mr. Begaye?

Ms. MCCARTHY. When was the first time?

Senator GARDNER. Yes.

Ms. McCarthy. I believe on August 11th, but I could be wrong.

Senator Gardner. When was the first time you spoke with the representative of the Southern Ute Tribe?

Ms. McCarthy. August 12th. I am sorry, that was August 11th.

Senator Gardner. August 11th. Thank you.

Did the agency follow the National Contingency Plan for notification and implementation of its response regarding the Gold King Mine spill?

Ms. McCarthy. I believe that it did.

Senator Gardner. Did the EPA know it was likely feasible the waters impounded behind the Gold King Mine would blowout?

Ms. McCarthy. That was one of the reasons we were there, so yes.

Senator Gardner. What preliminary actions were being taken to prevent that?

Ms. McCarthy. The actual action we were going up to do was to try to relieve the pressure by removing some of the water behind the adit, the blockage in the adit, and then to address through a trench an ability to treat the water that was coming out.

Senator Gardner. We do not know and that is what the review is telling us, whether that was adequate for the safe remediation to take place to prevent the blowout in the first place? That is what the review will show?

Ms. McCarthy. The review will take a look at the whole thing. The internal review already took a look at what factors were considered that made both the State of Colorado and EPA come to the conclusion that it was low or no pressure.

Obviously that was an inaccurate conclusion. There are a lot of series of recommendations on how we may look at this differently, but I fully expect the DOI will go into a lot more detail and that is really where we will see whether they did due diligence and acted appropriately or whether they could have or should have known better.

Senator Gardner. Why did it take so long for the estimate of the 1 million gallons to move to the 3 million gallons after the blowout?

Ms. McCarthy. Obviously the 1 million gallons was not determined through any mechanical measure. The USGS came in and looked at stream gauge data and that is where it went to 3 million gallons. Obviously we were wrong and underestimated the original spill. Why there was a delay in that, I do not know.

Senator Gardner. Was the EPA aware there was a stream gauge in place?

Ms. McCarthy. I do not know the answer to that. USGS is a partner of ours. They do stream gauges, so we had to know there were some in the area.

Senator Gardner. There should not have been any doubt as to whether it was 1 million or 3 million gallons?

Ms. McCarthy. We were not relying on that to make the first estimate. Why, I do not know but I certainly can look into it.

Senator Gardner. Is that part of the review as well?

Ms. McCarthy. We will make it part of the review and I will get you the information.

Senator GARDNER. The EPA employees and contractors carrying out the work, could you describe the expertise of the employees carrying out the work at the Gold King Mine?

Ms. MCCARTHY. There was an on-scene coordinator who has worked for many years for the agency. He is a mining engineer. He was overseeing the contractor. The work plan itself was developed, as I said, with the State of Colorado Division of Reclamation, Mining and Safety, as well as our team in Region 8.

We had that work plan reviewed by the Animas River stakeholder group. We also went to two public hearings with it.

The work was carried out on-site under the auspices of our on-site coordinator. The State of Colorado Mining Division folks were at the site, left a little bit before the spill occurred and it is my understanding they were still in the area and helped us with the first, initial notifications.

The work was, again, led by and carried out by our on-scene coordinator in accordance with the work plan that was designed.

Senator GARDNER. Was there was no cell phone coverage where this occurred? Did they have the ability to make contact if there was a blowout?

Ms. MCCARTHY. This came up at the prior hearing and I will have to get back to you as to whether or not there was cell phone coverage or not. I do know they reached their Colorado colleagues who were in the area and they were the ones who went down and made some of the first notifications.

Senator GARDNER. What is the EPA's legal obligation in current policies, guidelines on reporting and release of hazardous substances?

Ms. MCCARTHY. We would follow the same process as everybody else.

Senator GARDNER. Were those followed?

Ms. MCCARTHY. We would have to notify. Actually, the State of Colorado made two calls that I understand first was to our region and to the National Response Center.

Senator GARDNER. To the best of your knowledge, the EPA followed those guidelines?

Ms. MCCARTHY. To the best of my knowledge.

Senator GARDNER. EPA's legal obligations and current policies are what when it comes to contacting tribal, State and local governing agencies? What are those policies?

Ms. MCCARTHY. That we should do it as quickly as possible.

Senator GARDNER. In this instance, you believe it was done as quickly as possible?

Ms. MCCARTHY. No, I do not. I think it could have been done more quickly which is why we are reviewing all of that.

Senator GARDNER. Who was responsible for that lack of timeliness?

Ms. MCCARTHY. I did not want to misstate this. The regional contingency plan is what dictates how we notify downstream. In the State, we work in collaboration with the State to do that.

I think the difficulty or what we need to improve on here is that I think they looked at the State of Colorado first and did not go downstream until a bit later. There was no reason that I can think of that we would not have realized that it was a much larger issue than the State of Colorado.

Senator GARDNER. Who was the individual who made that decision then, to not go any further?

Ms. McCARTHY. I do not know whether that decision was made or we failed to make the decision to go further.

Senator GARDNER. Mr. Chairman, my time has expired. I have a lot further questions but I will have plenty of opportunity.

The CHAIRMAN. Thank you, Senator Gardner.

Senator Heinrich?

Senator HEINRICH. Actually, I want to follow up a bit on this line of questioning regarding further downstream.

If I understand your testimony correctly, there was a heavy equipment contractor on-site who was a contractor but there was also EPA supervision at the site as well?

Ms. McCARTHY. Yes.

Senator HEINRICH. Did that arrangement in any way contribute to or complicate the response in this case? If you would, also talk a little bit about whether your finding that the fact that this was at the convergence of effectively three EPA regions and how that may have complicated the response. We found that to be cumbersome and confusing in the early hours.

Also, can you tell us what you have learned about how to deal with an issue that may quickly migrate from one EPA region to multiple EPA regions?

Ms. McCARTHY. Let me answer your first question. I feel it would be inappropriate for me to give a judgment on your question about what contributed at the site because clearly that is something I would not have an independent understanding of and why we want DOI to do a job with the Army Corps and others to independently look at this.

Our challenge is to wait until October so that then we can take action beyond that. In the meantime, I have put in place a hiatus on any similar activities so that I will learn the lessons when they come and we will take advantage of those. I will take action, if warranted, in any disciplinary action as well. We will see where it comes out and act appropriately.

In terms of the notification, one of the things we did as well was to tell people to stop and take a look at what happened and revise their contingency plan accordingly. I have no doubt that there are difficulties for EPA and others when we shift from tribal and State lands. I think that may have added to the confusion. I cannot say whether it did but I do know it should not have.

We do regional plans, we do area plans and those should have kicked in. Part of the challenge is to stop worrying about redundancy and make sure that if people get five calls, it is better than getting none. I think there was some of that gap that played into this that should never happen again.

Senator HEINRICH. I would urge some level of specificity on that issue as we move forward. If you could get that for us, it would be very helpful. You have one region in Colorado. As this migrates to New Mexico, you have another region. As it enters the Navajo Nation, you have a third region.

I think that made things very cumbersome in the early hours to figure out who, municipal, tribal and other officials, including our office, should be communicating with. Unfortunately, until we find a mechanism for cleaning this stuff up and actually get serious about issues like 1872 Mining Act reform, I can pretty much guarantee that someday this is going to happen again because it has happened in the past. The 1979 spill was even worse.

Ms. McCarthy. We should not rely on the incredibly quick response we have received from every one of the States and the tribes to make sure that this did not go anywhere. I just cannot thank them enough. I do not expect them to have patience about this at all and neither do I.

Senator Heinrich. Shifting gears a bit to the issue of Superfund and the National Priorities List, one of the issues that has contributed to the sensitivity Senator Bennet mentioned and what I would call a bit of sense of Superfund stigma is the idea that a Superfund designation would have a negative impact on tourism.

I can say the experience in New Mexico with Questa has not necessarily lined up with that. We have seen other places like the jackpile mine in Moab, Utah where that did not have a negative impact on the brand of outdoor recreation that is obviously important in southwestern Colorado as much as it is for the region and in New Mexico and Arizona as well.

Is that something you are having conversations with the local communities about? I would urge you, as Senator Bennet said, to talk to the local communities. I would say not just everyone in Colorado but everyone in the watershed.

If we do a Superfund designation in this case and move forward putting this area on the National Priorities List, which I believe is warranted, the reality is, as we have seen from the testimony today, the impacts of action or inaction, in this case, are not in a single State but in multiple States and tribal nations.

Ms. McCarthy. I appreciate that. Thank you.

The Chairman. Thank you, Senator Heinrich.

Senator Hoeven?

STATEMENT OF HON. JOHN HOEVEN,
U.S. SENATOR FROM NORTH DAKOTA

Senator Hoeven. Thank you, Mr. Chairman.

Administrator, I am concerned about the issue of accountability as well. Can you tell us at this point who at the agency is responsible for the spill?

Ms. McCarthy. The Environmental Protection Agency is what I know, sir. We are going to wait for the Department of the Interior because that is an independent review that I think has the most value about understanding whether or not people did what they were supposed to do.

If you read our internal review, it is very clear, as are the documents going onto that site and the work plan, that the biggest concern was the blowout. People anticipated that blowout was inevitable which is why we were there trying to find a way to relieve that pressure.

Senator Hoeven. This long after the spill, you are still trying to determine who is accountable for the spill?

Ms. McCarthy. We certainly know who was at the site and I certainly what accountability means because EPA is taking the steps we should take to be accountable.

Senator Hoeven. What actions have you taken to make sure that a similar spill or accident does not occur in the future? If you do not know who is accountable, how can you take steps for the future?

Ms. McCarthy. That is the reason for the Department of the Interior review, to tell us what went wrong. I have made sure that there is no ongoing work that could be subject to the same kinds of problems.

Senator Hoeven. What perspective does this incident give you and the agency in terms of how you enforce the regulations that you have relative to other companies, whether we are talking about WOTUS, CO_2 rules, ozone, methane, all these rules that you are bringing out and the companies you regulate, what perspective does this incident give you and the agency in terms of how you deal with those companies?

Ms. McCarthy. Senator, we are holding ourselves to the same standards to which we hold the private sector which is that when you are doing remediation efforts like this, which we know are difficult and at times, dangerous, your job is to do a work plan that is solid, that gets the range of advice you need which I think we can all agree we had lots of private discussions about this.

The first order of business when something like this happens is to keep your people at the site safe, to stop the spill as quickly as you can, and then to clean it up. Those are the steps we ask of anyone outside. Those are the steps we are taking ourselves.

There are times in the private sector when there are fines involved in these types of activities but that is when they are actually operating or conducting actions not in concert with orders or other executive actions.

Senator Hoeven. You are getting a lot of questions about accountability today and not providing specific answers on accountability. I will give you another example.

You recently went out with CO_2 rules. For some States like ours, you said, you are going to have to make an 11 percent reduction. Then without bringing out new proposed rules, you change it to a 45 percent reduction. Where is the accountability?

In other words, you demand accountability from the companies you regulate. Where is the accountability at your agency?

I also called you on the phone and asked you personally to meet with our industry. You said you would. Now I understand we will be meeting with your staff and not with you. I think accountability calls for you to step up and address these issues.

Ms. McCarthy. Senator, I am happy to talk to you when you are visiting. I was not aware of it but I will see if I cannot take care of it.

Senator Hoeven. I think it goes to the underlying accountability. I know you require accountability when you are dealing with companies that have to follow your rules. We are looking for the same accountability from the agency.

Ms. McCarthy. And you should.

Senator Hoeven. Thank you.

The CHAIRMAN. Senator Heitkamp?

STATEMENT OF HON. HEIDI HEITKAMP,
U.S. SENATOR FROM NORTH DAKOTA

Senator HEITKAMP. Thank you, Mr. Chairman.

One of the reasons why we are in this room is because this has had a very, very dramatic effect on the downstream tribes who rely on this water. Water is king in the West and we all know that. Anytime you take away a water supply or threaten a water supply, you threaten the economics of every entity that uses that water.

In our case, we are very concerned about the impact this has had on Native American tribes downstream, the impact it has had on their culture, the impact on their ability to do the traditional things they hope to do as Senator Udall discussed earlier.

I do not think you can be very proud if you read the testimony of the tribal members who will testify today because they talk repeatedly about a culture of distrust with the EPA. I want to know what you are going to do to change that culture of distrust.

How are you going to not just say we are going to look at this and see how we can do better, but how you can change that cultural piece that is going to tell these tribal members and leaders you are a full-on partner and not ignoring the fact that they have a stake in this game?

Ms. McCARTHY. We are having ongoing dialogue, Senator, and I appreciate it. There is no question that when a spill like this happens, the credibility of this agency suffers, not just in terms of its relationship with the tribes, but all of the people that we serve.

We are going to be accountable. We are going to get the data that we need to do that. We are going to continue to work with the tribes.

We recently responded to some of their most recent requests about supporting third parties to come in. If they do not trust us, I am fine with supporting third party sampling or verification of our sample results.

I have asked what we can do to establish a path forward on the cultural damage this has caused. I am more than willing to sit down with the tribes and go through their list of what they think is necessary for us to repair the damage this spill caused, not just physically but the emotional and cultural damage this has brought with it. Nobody would want to do that more than I would.

Senator HEITKAMP. One of the situations we recently had was a fire which was lit by the Forest Service and lots of apologies at the beginning but when it came time to file the torts claim, somehow magically there was no negligence, magically whatever culpability and damages as a result of that culpability dissipates and puts huge burdens on the victims to pursue some kind of claim.

I want a commitment from you that will not happen in this case, that there will be a honest, forthright evaluation of what those damages are and there is going to be the ability for these tribal entities and the downstream entities to actually get compensated for the damage caused by EPA.

Ms. McCARTHY. I will do the very best I can.

Senator HEITKAMP. Everyone says they will do their very best. Frequently when lawyers get involved, you and I share that label, we sometimes forget that the rest of the world can see things through a lens that is different than a legal lens.

Do not put these tribal entities, tribal leaders and their tribes through the process simply to forestall compensation for the damages. For me, that is a huge part of how you can build that trust which is take responsibility, we can talk about firing people and hopefully, as you go through that process, you will find people who will be culpable.

The other piece of this in terms of accountability is compensation. Please, do not put these downstream victims in the spot where they need to be begging for what is fair and just in this case.

Ms. McCarthy. I hear you. Thank you, Senator.

The Chairman. Thank you, Senator Heitkamp.

Senator Daines?

STATEMENT OF HON. STEVE DAINES,
U.S. SENATOR FROM MONTANA

Senator Daines. Thank you, Mr. Chairman.

Administrator McCarthy, in November 2009, President Obama issued a memo reiterating his Administration's commitment to Executive Order 13175 requiring all Federal agencies to engage in ''regular and meaningful consultation and collaboration with tribal officials in the development of Federal policies that have tribal implications and the Federal agencies are responsible for strengthening the government-to-government relationship between the United States and Indian tribes.''

I was struck when Senator Gardner asked question about when the Navajo President was notified. The spill occurred on August 5. I understand you did not engage him until six days later on August 11.

My question is, if this spill had been with Canada or Mexico, do you think it would have taken six days before you picked up the phone to call one of the leaders in either Canada or Mexico?

Ms. McCarthy. President Begaye?

Senator Daines. Correct, President Begaye. Senator Gardner asked when you contacted him. It was six days after the spill. The spill was on August 5th. You said you called him on August 11th, six days later.

My question is had this been with Canada or Mexico, would it have taken six days for the head of the EPA to contact the leaders in those respective countries?

Ms. McCarthy. I am hoping that you understand we were in the middle of an emergency. The president was engaged in this at high levels in the agency. Did I have a direct conversation with him? I do not believe so.

Senator Daines. By Executive Order 12175 and the way we think about our tribes and their sovereignty, this is a government-to-government relationship.

Ms. McCarthy. Yes.

Senator Daines. Why would the tribes be receiving much less attention and care than the leader of one of our neighboring countries? That is my question. Why?

Ms. McCarthy. You have made a very legitimate point. Point taken, sir.

Senator DAINES. Thank you.

This is not the first time I have heard about difficult cooperation between the EPA and Indian tribes. As you and I discussed in a Senate Appropriations Committee hearing in April, the Crow Nation of Montana is very, very frustrated with the amount of consultation that has been done regarding EPA's Clean Power Plan.

In fact, I had a field hearing on April 8th. I invited the EPA. The field hearing was on the Crow Reservation. I invited EPA to participate in that hearing and they declined. Eventually, a member from the State EPA of Montana came and sat in the audience.

I see a systemic failure in my view of the EPA engaging and treating these tribes with the dignity and respect they deserve. In fact, at the Appropriations Committee hearing in April, you mentioned interest in resolving the Crow Tribe's concerns with the Clean Power Plan.

Ms. McCARTHY. Yes.

Senator DAINES. To my knowledge, given the Crow and Midwest utilities, the EPA has completely failed at meaningful consultation with the Crow tribe.

It is my understanding the Navajo Nation had a similar concern with consultation with the EPA during development of the Clean Power Plan. In fact, I am looking forward to hearing from Navajo Nation President Begaye discuss this on the next panel.

Given the concerns of the Crow Nation and the Navajo Nation, which face some of the highest unemployment rates in the Country, in Crow Indian Country, it is 47 percent unemployment and without these natural resource jobs, their unemployment rate goes north of 80 percent.

My question is, is your agency upholding its obligations under Executive Order 13175?

Ms. McCARTHY. I believe we are, sir.

Senator DAINES. Let me just say with the six day lag with President Begaye, that was a failure. Observing what is going on with the Clean Power Plan, there have been failures with the EPA communicating. We probably have a difference of opinion, I do not think you have.

In fact, there is a saying in Montana, we say ''all hat and no cattle.''

Ms. McCARTHY. Cattle?

Senator DAINES. That means folks come in from out of State and wear a big hat, talk big, but there is no substance. They are full of big talk but lacking action is what that means. This my concern with the EPA as I hear about these things as we sit in these hearings but look at what is going on in the lives of real people with real challenges. I am seeing a big disconnect.

Ms. McCARTHY. Thank you, sir.

Senator DAINES. Thank you.

The CHAIRMAN. Senator Lankford.

STATEMENT OF HON. JAMES LANKFORD,
U.S. SENATOR FROM OKLAHOMA

Senator LANKFORD. Administrator, thank you for walking through the multiple hearings you have been in to be able to walk through this as well. I appreciate your getting a chance to walk through this. Most everything has been asked and I want some clarification.

You talked several times about the accountability and that the report will come from Interior to kind of identify where we are with accountability. When will that report be done?

Ms. McCarthy. It is scheduled to be completed in October.

Senator Lankford. At that time, once that comes in, obviously EPA will engage in trying to apply whatever that accountability may be, including I would hope with the tribal leaders and tribes as well.

As the Senators asked before, the tort relationships and the responsibility and accountability then are ongoing. My concern is with the statement the river has now returned to pre-spill levels which almost sounds like everything is fine, everybody leave.

My hope is that is now where we are going, that we are just like it was a dirty river before, it is still a dirty river, we are moving.

Ms. McCarthy. There are two ways in which that is not the case. One is that we are working on a long range plan. The sediments are a concern. That is one of the major concerns you will hear from President Begaye. We recognize that we have an ongoing challenge there. We also have the larger challenge of what to do across the watershed at the top of the Animas River.

There are two large actions, one of which is within the control of EPA, which is getting a monitoring plan that everyone is comfortable with that will keep us active and engaged in that region in a way that all of us can recognize we are doing the job we are supposed to do, not just short or long term.

Senator Lankford. Thank you.

Let me ask a couple questions for the record and follow up later on some of these conversations. Just so you know, they are going to be slightly off topic.

On April 27th of this year, the Army Corps of Engineers wrote a memo to EPA saying they believe certain aspects of the Waters of the U.S. rule would not hold up to Supreme Court scrutiny. They wrote that to EPA. We have that document and that memo. We do not have the response from EPA where they responded, no, here is why we think it does. We have only the final rule that came out.

I would like a copy of that response. We have one side of a conversation but do not have the other side of the conversation. Would it be possible to get the other side of that conversation, the response, if I provided you the April 27th memo from the Army Corps of Engineers so you can see exactly what it was?

Ms. McCarthy. I will follow up on that. I may not have the exact memo. We will track it down.

Senator Lankford. That would be great.

The other issue deals with renewable fuel standards. This is something we have talked about before. November 30th is coming quickly. Do you still feel you are on schedule to release the 14, 15 and 16 RFS mandates by November 30th?

Ms. McCarthy. Yes, sir.

Senator Lankford. The ozone rule that is coming out obviously has been sent over to OMB to my understanding from EPA?

Ms. McCarthy. Yes, sir

Senator LANKFORD. When this comes out and the final piece is out, I would like to be able to get a copy of what your proposal was to OMB when you originally sent it over. I know there will be some conversation of where it went, what they are going to do from there, but the history of the decision-making process.

This will affect my State dramatically. It will affect the whole Country pretty dramatically.

Ms. MCCARTHY. You will be able to see that. I was asking because I am aware that when a rule is finalized, that information becomes part of the record. I am not exactly sure when.

Senator LANKFORD. The history of it will be important to us because again all of us will be dramatically affected by this. It also affects the RFS since obviously ethanol in production creates more ozone. When you have a decrease in ozone requirement and an increase in RFS requirement, you have EPA doing things in conflict and you cannot make it.

We want to get that for the record and go from there.

Mr. Chairman, thank you.

The CHAIRMAN. Thank you, Senator Lankford.

Thank you very much, Administrator McCarthy.

There being no other questions, we know you have another appointment. We will move to the second panel.

We will recess for five minutes.

Ms. MCCARTHY. Thank you so much, Mr. Chairman.

The CHAIRMAN. Thanks for being here.

[Recess.]

The CHAIRMAN. We have a distinguished panel. We will start with Russell Begaye, President of the Navajo Nation. We will also have the Honorable James ''Mike'' Olguin, Tribal Council Member of the Southern Ute Indian Tribe; Douglas Holtz-Eakin, President of the American Action Forum, Washington, D.C.; Dr. David C. Weindorf, Associate Dean for Research, Department of Plant and Soil Sciences, Texas Tech University, Lubbock, Texas, thank you for joining us; and Mr. Gilbert Harrison, a rancher and irrigator of the Navajo Nation in New Mexico. Thank you also for being with us. I would like to start with President Begaye.

If everyone could please keep your comments to about five minutes that will give more time for questioning.

President Begaye.

STATEMENT OF HON. RUSSELL BEGAYE, PRESIDENT, NAVAJO NATION

Mr. BEGAYE. Good afternoon, Chairman Barrasso, Vice Chairman Tester and members of the Committee. Thank you, Senators Udall, Heinrich and McCain.

Thank you for your leadership in this hearing, appearing in person and for sending staff to investigate the area.

My name is Russell Begaye of the Ashiihii Ta'neeszahnii clan. I am the President of the Navajo Nation.

I am grateful for this opportunity to address this prestigious group of Senators and leaders. Thank you for helping to make right an injustice that has occurred on our land and to our river.

August 11th will always be remembered on our Nation as a day when the Navajo way of life for our people was disrupted through the negligence of the United States Environmental Protection Agency.

On that day, over 3 million gallons of yellow contaminants rushed down the Animas River to our river, the San Juan. The San Juan has been the lifeline for our people for centuries. Water is sacred and the river is the life for all of us. It is who we are. It breathes. It provides. It nourishes. It defines us.

The San Juan has always been a source of sustenance for our ranchers and farmers. It provides us with healthy organic food, drinking water for our people, feed for our livestock, herbal medicine for our ceremonies and has been a source of enjoyment for our children.

Today, we are afraid to use the river, to use it for drinking, for our livestock, and to irrigate our farms. I have stood in the fields with our farmers as they shed tears over their crops. For them, the crops are more than income, but are a source of pride and joy, crops they share with their neighbors, their children, and their grandchildren. The spirit of my people has been greatly impacted by this negligent act.

Yes, we have been told by the EPA that the river is back to its precondition levels but we do not know what precondition levels means. Simply, we do not trust the EPA. Why? They did not inform the Nation of the accident until two days after the blowout. I believe the only reason they finally informed the Navajo Nation is because you cannot hide an accident when the rivers turn orange.

When we first received notice, they told us it was 1 million gallons of contaminants that was released from the mine but later, they changed it to 3 million gallons. Since then, it has neared 30 million gallons.

At a public hearing, the USEPA representative said the water was churning up at the base of the mountain but when the vice president and went to the mouth of the mine to visually investigate, we were stunned to see the yellow river.

I even showed the USEPA officials a picture I had just taken a few hours before of the toxic waters that were still pouring out of the mine and it was yellow.

The last straw was when USEPA gave my people 20 million gallon water tanks for relief. Those tanks were tainted with oil. I directly asked the USEPA about the tainted tanks. They vehemently denied that they had oily substances in them.

They said, it is only used for clean drinking water but when I personally went to one tank, put my hand into the intake valve of that tank, my hand came out blackened with oil. They expected us to give that tainted water to our livestock and crops.

Let me again say, the Navajo Nation does not trust the USEPA. We expect them to be held fully accountable for what they have done to my people and to all the people who live along both the San Juan and Animas Rivers.

I am not just speaking today for my people but all peoples whose souls are hurting from what should have been an avoidable, negligent act. Today is our greatest time of need with our people struggling for water for their animals, livestock and irrigation. The USEPA has abandoned us.

The water tanks are being pulled out, feed for our livestock has stopped. Last Friday, Ms. McCarthy and I spoke on the phone and she was unaware that the USEPA had stopped providing resources to the Navajo Nation. She said, I did not know that we stopped giving water. I did not know that we stopped giving hay.

As EPA Administrator, how does she not know that this was happening? The orders to leave our Nation came from her regional directors. This just adds to the culture of distrust they have created.

What my people need first and foremost is compensation and need it now. The farmers cannot wait three months later or even a year from now. Our farmers have spent monies they do not have and are expected to purchase materials, haul water and buy hay for their livestock.

Our farmers and ranchers still need hay and water. EPA has pulled out. BIA has expended all of their funds. We are now taking monies from our emergency account to help our people.

I am saying that today I want this Committee to stand with us and make sure the EPA pays for what it has done to my people, to my Nation.

Thank you.

[The prepared statement of Mr. Begaye follows:]

PREPARED STATEMENT OF HON. RUSSELL BEGAYE, PRESIDENT, NAVAJO NATION

I. Introduction

Yá'át'ééh (hello) Chairman Barrasso, Vice-Chairman Tester, and Members of the Committee, my name is Russell Begaye. I am the President of the Navajo Nation. I was raised on a farm along the San Juan River in Shiprock, New Mexico, one of the communities directly impacted by the subject of this hearing. Thank you for this opportunity to testify before your Committee on a matter that is of utmost importance to the Navajo Nation.

As you know, on Wednesday August 5, 2015, the United States Environmental Protection Agency (USEPA), and other parties, caused a massive release of toxic contaminants from the Gold King Mine into Cement Creek. The toxic sludge—which included harmful contaminants such as lead and arsenic—flowed south from the Cement Creek into the Animas River, then into the San Juan River (River), a major water source for the Navajo Nation. The San Juan River flows through 215 miles of some of the richest farmland in the Nation's territory, and provides much of the Nation's northern border. The impact to the Navajo Nation from this drastic release is compounded by the fact that much of this portion of the River is slower moving than upstream.

Today, in the brief time I have, I would like to cover only a few critical areas of concern for the Navajo people. The critical areas of concern are as follows:

- The USEPA's, among others', mishandling of the spill and the emergency response; USEPA's lack of timely notice, transparency, and consistency; and the resulting culture of distrust;
- History of contamination of the San Juan River and the need for cleanup;
- Our preliminary findings on the short-term and long-term impacts of the spill on the Navajo people and environment, including economic, health, cultural, and spiritual impacts.

To address the serious impacts of this spill and the continued threat to the Navajo people from future contamination, we request the following:

- Resources from USEPA, FEMA and BIA to address the immediate emergency;
- Assurances that USEPA will fairly and timely compensate the affected farmers and livestock owners for their damages, both in the near term and long term.
- Resources to conduct our own water, sediment, and soil monitoring, and recognized authority for the Navajo Nation EPA to do the necessary work.
- That the USEPA address all the contamination that is flowing into the River.

- Resources to address near- and intermediate-term environmental and health impacts;
- Resources to study and address the long-term environmental and health impacts of the spill, and to restore the River to a safe and healthy state; and
- A fair and independent assessment of the role USEPA, and others, played in the events leading up to the Gold King Mine spill, and the establishment of a different lead agency.

It is important to realize that in addition to the many known and yet unknown physical, chemical, biological, and economic effects of this spill, this spill has taken a cultural and spiritual toll on our society, disrupting our *hozho*. *Hozho* encompasses beauty, order, and harmony, and expresses the idea of striving to maintain balance in the Navajo universe. The trauma from this spill will be felt for years to come, and we need immediate and sustained help to restore the balance for our people.

II. The USEPA'S Mishandling of the Spill and Creation of a Culture of Distrust

The NNEPA works in close partnership with USEPA to facilitate the Nation's twelve environmental programs, which are largely, if not completely, funded by the USEPA. A good and close working relationship with USEPA has always been critical to the success of the NNEPA. However, recent events relating to this spill have led to a complete shift in that relationship as USEPA has sought to quiet our legitimate concerns, and has made repeated missteps in its response efforts. We have serious concerns about the strong conflict of interest USEPA has with respect to this investigation and the emergency response necessary. No other environmental bad actor would be given leeway to investigate itself and determine to what extent it will be held accountable. We are encouraged that USEPA's Office of Inspector General will be reviewing this incident, but we believe another agency should take the lead on the on-ground response, and an independent body should conduct the investigation.

To begin with, the USEPA inexplicably delayed notification of the spill to the Navajo Nation. The spill occurred the morning of August 5, 2015, but the Nation was not informed of the release until August 6, a full day later, and not even by the USEPA but by the State of New Mexico. It took the USEPA almost two full days to notify us. We view this as a violation of the government-to-government relationship between the Federal Government and the Navajo Nation.

The USEPA also demonstrated a complete lack of transparency. Our initial warning from USEPA was of an "acid mine drainage spill in the Animas River north of Durango" of "[a]pproximately 1 [million] gallons." USEPA's initial focus appeared to be on pH levels. This served to downplay the magnitude of risk to human and animal health, and later reports by USEPA of released contaminants were incomplete. The media was receiving faster and fuller information from USEPA than the Navajo Nation. For example, the New York Times reported the spill hours before USEPA provided the Nation with notice of the spill. And media sources reported that USEPA confirmed the presence of arsenic on Friday, August 7, whereas USEPA still had not reported the presence of arsenic to the Nation even by Sunday, August 9.

USEPA on Friday, August 7 informed the Nation that "the water in Cement Creek and the Animas River near Silverton is clearing," but the Vice-President and I nonetheless made plans to travel to the Gold King Mine Sunday to assess the situation for ourselves.[1] We requested a tour from USEPA, but faced immediate resistance. USEPA staff indicated they would only take us to the confluence of Cement Creek with the Animas River in Silverton, Colorado, but the water at the confluence remained bright orange. It did not appear to be "clearing." We thus urged USEPA to take us to the point of release. They again refused, this time compromising by offering to take us to the treatment pools below the mine adit. We finally convinced them to take us within a half-mile of the point of release. We walked the rest of the way to the point of release. There we saw a completely unblocked mine adit with an estimated 550 gallon per minute flow of bright, opaque orange liquid pouring forth. We have since learned that prior to the blocking of the nearby Sunnyside Mine and the Red and Bonita Mine, Gold King Mine was releasing water at only 7 gallons per minute.[2] We took video footage and photos at the point of release and

---

[1] E-mail from Harry Allen, Chief, Emergency Response Section, USEPA Region 9, to Russell Begaye, President, Navajo et al (Aug. 7, 2015, 11:58 PT) (on file with NNDOJ).
[2] *http://fox6now.com/2015/08/13/gold-king-mine-owner-i-foresaw-disaster-before-epa-spill-into-animas-river-in-colorado/*

shared these with the public. This appeared to be the first time USEPA Region 9 staff visited the point of release.

While USEPA was slow in notifying the Nation of the initial spill and its associated risks, it was quick in dispatching staff to Navajo communities to hand out Standard Form 95 and encouraging members of the Navajo Nation to fill out forms to expedite settlement of their claims under the Federal Tort Claims Act and apparently to obtain releases from members of the Navajo Nation. But this was only after I announced that the Navajo Nation would be suing the USEPA and other liable parties for the spill. The Navajo Nation Attorney General reviewed the form and identified plain and clear language on the form asserting that individuals submitting the forms would be filing the forms in pursuit of "FULL SATISFACTION AND FINAL SETTLEMENT" of their claims for damages and injuries that yet remain unknown.

This presented our people with a difficult choice. The economics of farming makes the cashing out of harvests time-critical. Our farming families were expecting to sell their harvests along a predictable timeline that was disrupted by the closing of the San Juan River to irrigation use. They relied on the predictability of this timeline to defer bills and expenses until harvest time. Now that time is passing, and many of them need their anticipated harvest returns immediately to catch up on bills and to buy school clothes, among other things. Yet if they fill out Standard Form 95 and receive a settlement check, they may not be able to defer cashing that check while they wait for additional damages or injuries to accrue. I, along with the Vice-President and Attorney General, have thus asked USEPA for an interim claims process that will allow for ongoing claims filings, and our Attorney General has asked for a U.S. Attorney General opinion confirming that the filing of Standard Form 95 and the settling of a claim filed under that form or process does not in fact fully satisfy and settle the claim. None of this has happened while the Navajo people continue to suffer. Despite our requests, the USEPA has yet to confirm to us that it will fully and fairly address all damages and injuries to members of the Navajo Nation who have been impacted by the spill.

These instances—but a few among many—have led to distrust by the Navajo Nation towards USEPA, both among our farmers and our leadership. The NNEPA, in contrast, continues to have the trust of our farmers and our leadership. Despite the NNEPA's limited resources, we turn to the NNEPA for honest data assessments and technical answers.

III. History of Contamination of the San Juan River and the Need for Cleanup

This incident is one of many where responsible parties have contaminated Navajo land and water. I was born and raised in Shiprock, and as a child one summer, I once saw hundreds of dead fish floating down the San Juan River. We knew something was not right with all these dead fish in the River. But the next day we were back in the water, playing in it. There was no one to tell us to stay out of the water—that it was dangerous. We always wondered why all the fish died in the River, and it was not until USEPA Administrator Gina McCarthy visited Shiprock on August 13, that I learned the story of why this occurred. There is a 1.5 million ton uranium tailings pile above a floodplain feeding into the San Juan River in the middle of Shiprock. That summer, a dam holding a pool of tailing-contaminant filled water burst into the River. But no one told us what had happened. We cannot tolerate this contamination of our sacred lands.

Yet the recent spill threatens to recur, either from unsettling of contaminated sediment in our River waters, or from ongoing contaminated releases from upstream mines. USEPA stated early on that we will be dealing with the effects of USEPA's Gold King Mine chemical spill "for decades." Gold King Mine is just one of over 300 abandoned hardrock mines in the heavily contaminated 140-mile-area known as the Upper Animas Mining District (District). [3] The District includes private, federal, and state lands, and the town of Silverton. [4] Gold King Mine was twice considered for inclusion on the National Priorities List (NPL), both as part of the District, and as a narrower carve-out from the District, and the recent spill was preceded by two spills in the 1970s. We sent a letter to Administrator McCarthy on Monday, September 7, requesting that this District be made a Superfund site so that USEPA will make the cleanup and containment of the site a priority, and thereby protect us downstream communities.

The Mine's first Superfund site assessment was conducted in the 1990s, and the assessment concluded, "that water quality standards were not achieved" in the Dis-

---

[3] *http://www2.epa.gov/region8/upper-animas-mining-district*
[4] *http://www2.epa.gov/region8/upper-animas-mining-district.*

trict.[5] The assessment also identified "severe impacts [of the District] to aquatic life in the Upper Animas and its tributaries."[6] Despite the serious harm being caused by the District, USEPA postponed listing the District on the NPL in order to allow a "community-based collaborative effort" to clean up and mitigate harm from the District "as long as progress was being made to improve the water quality of the Animas River."[7]

Yet in 2005, the "water quality ha[d] declined significantly" in the area, and so in 2008, USEPA performed another NPL assessment, this time on the Upper Cement Creek alone.[8] The study again confirmed, "that the area would qualify for inclusion" on the NPL.[9] Despite the additional confirmation that the Mine area should be listed on the NPL, "EPA postponed efforts to include the area on the National Priorities List," again "after receiving additional community input."[10] USEPA's repeated denial of the facts with respect to the level of harm posed by the Gold King Mine and its surrounding mines has placed downstream jurisdictions such as the Nation at undue risk. This further contributes to a lack of trust in USEPA's ability to protect the health and well-being of Navajo people.

The threat of a spill from the District remains under the existing management scheme. The chemicals found in the District pose significant human health risk as they contain known carcinogens and elements, like lead and arsenic, that can affect major organ systems such as cardiovascular, respiratory, gastrointestinal and reproductive systems. The risks to the Navajo people are very real. Neither my people nor the other communities living near the rivers can tolerate a recurrence of the unprecedented damage caused by the Gold King Mine Spill.

Based on our extrapolation of known data, over 20 million gallons of aggregate contaminated flow has spilled from the Mine since August 5. If the USEPA does not address these sites through designation as a Superfund site, contaminants will continue to flow freely into the Nation's waters, and the concentration of contaminants in our waters will increase, extending the duration of exposure for our people, which is already significant now, even further into the future. Metals poison people slowly, and sediments eventually make their way downstream. We are thus gravely concerned that the metals coming from Gold King Mine and the District are making their way down to us, and will settle in our slow waters. We are also concerned that efforts to flush contaminants out of the Farmington area flushed contaminated sediments into our territory, and that those contaminants will remain here for a long time. We do not want our people to be poisoned, so we urge you to do what you can to help us secure NPL listing for the District.

IV. Short and Long-Term Impacts

The impacts of this spill, as well as the ongoing contamination from mines in the area, are devastating and myriad. The reliance of our people on the San Juan River and the significance of the River to our people cannot be overstated. The Navajo Nation as a whole is a largely agricultural society, and our people have traditionally farmed and ranched since pre-contact. The San Juan River Basin is a bastion for ancient Navajo seed strains that our people have carefully refined over centuries to thrive in our arid region. Farming and ranching are the backbone of our culture and economy, and are both heavily dependent on the San Juan River. Indeed, in our arid region with little water distribution infrastructure in place, our farmers rely heavily on the San Juan River and ditch irrigation practices to keep their fields hydrated and their crops growing. I want to lay out for the Committee some of the impacts of the contamination on the Navajo Nation. But I want to stress that, because of the historic and long-term nature of the contamination caused by the spill and the lack of full transparency, all of the economic, health, cultural, and other impacts to the Navajo people are not yet known.

First, our farmers and ranchers and our traditional people felt the most immediate impact from the spill. You can imagine the significant economic and emotional toll on our farming families, who mostly live on their farmlands and consume their crops as a matter of subsistence. These families have lost a significant portion of a full growing season's worth of work. Now these families have to look at their dead crops each day, and are constantly reminded of the loss.

---

[5] *http://www2.epa.gov/sites/production/files/2015-08/documents/goldkingminewatershedfactsheetbackground.pdfat2.*

[6] *http://www2.epa.gov/sites/production/files/2015-08/documents/goldkingminewatershedfactsheetbackground.pdfat2.*

[7] *Id.*

[8] *Id.*

[9] *Id.*

[10] *Id.*

As I visited farmers and ranchers, I saw a lot of farms where corn had not fully matured due to lack of water. As a result, the corn crops had only the stalk but no corn. The corn pollen that is so critical to everyday Navajo spiritual life did not develop properly for many of these crops. A lot of Navajo melons only grew to a fifth of their size. One family was forced to abandon all but a single acre of their 32-acre field, opting to save plants with cultural significance.

Second, the spill has already severely impacted our economy and may continue to do so for years to come. The Navajo Nation already faces a daunting unemployment rate of 42 percent. Yet along the San Juan River, many of our people are able to make a life for themselves and support their families through farming and ranching. Many of our farmers create additional economic value for themselves by carefully growing profitable organic crops, or raising grass-fed and organic beef or mutton product. Now their livelihoods have been significantly disrupted by the spill. Growing cycles and field rotations have been disrupted, and farmers who are used to producing their own farm goods will now need to buy fruits and vegetables for themselves, and hay and alfalfa for their livestock, to replace what was lost. Our farmers will also lose income from the expected sales that did not or will not occur. Even farmers who have been able to salvage their farm goods now face a stigma developing with respect to fruits and vegetables grown along the San Juan River. This triggers a cycle of economic losses for the community.

Third, the long-term health effects of the spill are ominous and not fully understood. Heavy metals like lead, arsenic and others that were discharged during the spill are known to be dangerous to humans, animals, and plants. These metals persist in the environment and are particularly harmful to fetuses and children. To provide a sense of the magnitude of exposure to these harmful metals just from the spill, one report of EPA data indicated that lead was found near the Cement Creek/Animas River confluence "at more than 200 times higher than the acute exposure limit for aquatic life, and 3,580 times higher than federal standards for human drinking water." And arsenic was found "more than 24 times the exposure limit for fish and 823 times the level for human ingestion."[11] Human consumption of farm products and livestock raised on contaminated water is therefore of grave concern. We are especially concerned about sheep because sheep liver and kidney are cultural delicacies, and are organs that are most likely to concentrate contaminants. In addition, long-term effects on wildlife that live in or rely on the River for water must be understood because we hunt and fish these animals to put food on our tables, and as part of our traditional cultural practices. Although USEPA has stated that surface water returned to its previous condition, many of the contaminants have merely settled to the bed of the River, and will be remobilized later during storm events, for example.

Fourth are the cultural and spiritual losses that we have sustained. Indeed, the Navajo Nation's impacts are felt most pointedly in the disruption of our cultural principle of *hozho,* which encompasses beauty, order, and harmony, and expresses the idea of striving to maintain balance in the Navajo universe. We connect to our land, our water, and each other through ceremonies and gatherings. We grow four types of corn, each used for a specific purpose in our ceremonies, and those seeds are protected by the strong culture of farming that has persisted in the San Juan River Basin. Navajo cornhusks are mixed with tobacco to create ceremonial smoke, and our corn pollen is used as an essential element in all Navajo ceremonies. One of our corn seed strains is utilized in our critical kinaalda ceremonies (the coming of age ceremonies for our women). We also grow an array of heirloom fruits and vegetables that our people eagerly anticipate selling and purchasing during our popular fair season each fall. Those fruits and vegetables are shared over family tables, and are a part of the cultural glue that keeps our families and way of life intact. Families travel for hours across the Nation to the San Juan River Basin to access these ingredients for our ceremonies and celebrations. But the spill destroyed many of these crops so critical to our prayers, ceremonies, and our way of life.

Fifth, the impairment of the River and the adverse impacts to our farmers and ranchers, and our community as a whole, will mark a moment of community trauma that will be endured for years to come. This new trauma will compound our already significant historical trauma, and raises new and troubling public health concerns. Already three suicides have occurred in the course of the last two weeks in affected communities along the River. Our Department of Health is researching the connection of the suicides to the spill, and we are concerned that these might be the first of a larger cluster. This tragedy affects all of our Nation because so many of us have relatives in Northern Navajo. Compounding this trauma, are the repeated response failures and withdrawals of aid (and blockage of aid) by USEPA, which have sent

---

[11] *http://m.startribune.com/nation/321518301.html*

a strong message to our people that Navajo lives don't matter, that our health and well-being don't matter, and that our way of life doesn't matter. We will be dealing with the effects of this spill for decades and rebuilding the shattered sense of self so many of our people are experiencing as a result of this disaster.

V. Significant Resource Needs

In light of the devastating impacts from this spill, both known and yet unknown, we need to act quickly and thoughtfully to protect our Navajo citizens, our natural resources, the Navajo way of life, and most importantly our future generations. We need assistance from the responsible parties to address the short- and long-term impacts, to make us whole, and to return the beauty and *hozho* to our River and our people. In addition to oversight and national attention, Congress can provide forward-thinking legislative solutions to some of these issues. We therefore ask for the following:

1. We continue to need resources from USEPA, FEMA and BIA to address the ongoing need. We still need continued delivery of water for both livestock and farming, as well as the delivery of hay to impacted ranchers. Farmers and livestock owners are essentially fed water from two point sources along the San Juan River. Although we have allowed the waterways to be opened for irrigation only, the farmers who are fed water from one point source have unanimously voted not to use the San Juan River water because they lost all faith in the USEPA's data. These farmers still need water for both their crops and livestock and hay for their penned livestock. The USEPA's actions in this matter have spread fear, and our farmers and ranchers should not be penalized for their lack of trust in the USEPA.

On the other point source, the water was reopened for irrigation purposes only. Based on the data samples our Navajo Nation Environmental Protection Agency has seen, the contaminant levels were still above Navajo standards and therefore the water is not safe for consumption by livestock. As such, livestock owners in the area need to pen up their animals in order to prevent them from drinking the River water. They will still need water delivery and hay for their penned livestock.

Even in light of the above, the USEPA has essentially withdrawn assistance. The Bureau of Indian Affairs has been helpful, but they had to pull out because they ran out of funds. FEMA has denied assistance to Navajo, deferring to USEPA as the lead response agency. As it currently stands, there are no federal services being provided to farmers and ranchers in the area. We as a Navajo Nation government, and our farmers and livestock owners, are left to deal with not only the contamination, but the financial and emotional mess left behind by the USEPA's actions. I ask, why should we bear that burden?

2. If USEPA will not continue its services to mitigate the harm to farmers and ranchers, we need assurances that they will fairly and fully compensate the affected farmers and livestock owners for their damages. Many farmers and ranchers have lost crops. Many have expended their own funds to try and mitigate their damages. Some have lost economic value of their goods, among a whole host of other possible damages. We are unsure as to whether the FTCA claim process will provide fair, full, and ongoing compensation to our people. As previously stated, we have asked USEPA for an interim claims process or a relief fund that will allow for ongoing claims and quick remuneration. And we have asked the U.S. Attorney General for an opinion confirming that the filing of Standard Form 95 and the settling of a claim filed under that form or process does not in fact fully satisfy and settle the claim as the plain language of the form and the FTCA itself indicates. Despite the urgency with which our people need to be compensated for their already experienced losses, to date we have received no response or confirmation from the USEPA or USDOJ.

3. We need resources to conduct our own water, sediment, and soil monitoring, and authority for the NNEPA to do the necessary work. Due to our lack of trust in the USEPA and the conflict of interest that exists with the USEPA, we want to be able to monitor their work and confirm their results. We will require an on-site lab, and additional staffing to manage the sampling and lab performance. We are already expanding our scope of work into the realm of sediment testing, but testing and lab work is expensive, so we need additional funding to facilitate that work. This will enable us to provide our farmers and our leaders with the answers they deserve, and with answers they can trust.

4. The U.S. Environmental Protection Agency needs to clean up all the contamination that is flowing into the River. As we have discovered, along with the Gold

King Mine, there are many hundreds of hardrock mines along the River that continually release contaminants into the River. We suspect that the volume of contaminants they release over time is much greater in magnitude than this latest burst from the Gold King Mine. USEPA needs to develop a plan to clean up these sources of contaminants, share their plan, and implement and complete that plan. We request, as part of the plan, that USEPA designate these mines as superfund sites.

5. *We need resources to address near- and intermediate-term impacts.* We need assistance to create redundant and auxiliary water supplies, at least two treatment plants, additional drilling for wells, repair of windmills and new reservoirs to guard against the negative impacts of future contamination. Until there is a plan in place from the USEPA that would prevent future contamination of the San Juan River, and that plan is implemented, we need these water supplies and reservoirs in case we need to shut off water from the River again. For the sake of our people and our Nation, we hope we do not ever have to do that again, but for now, that risk remains. We also need treatment plants to filter out contaminants to make the water safe for human, animal and agricultural consumption, including a water treatment plant at the head of our waters in the communities of Upper Fruitland and Shiprock.

6. *We need resources to study and address the long-term health, economic and environmental impacts of the spill and to return the River to a safe and healthy state.* While long-term health and economic impacts have not yet been quantified, we believe they will be substantial. We will need assistance monitoring health impacts, including mental health impacts, as well as the resources necessary to fund this monitoring effort and to fund treatment, if necessary. Extensive planning and study will be needed to return the San Juan River to a safe and healthy state.

7. *We demand a fair and independent assessment of the USEPA's and others' role in the spill, and the establishment of a different lead agency.* Since they were the cause of this contamination, we have serious concerns about the strong conflict of interest USEPA has with respect to this investigation and the emergency response. An independent body should conduct the investigation, and FEMA should take over as lead responding agency.

8. *We ask that Congress revisit this important issue and the federal response in six months.* This complex issue will not disappear overnight for the Navajo people; we request Congress hold another hearing in six months ensure the Federal Government, starting with the responsible party, the USEPA, has made sufficient progress.

Ahéhee.' Thank you for your time and attention to this important issue.

Senator MCCAIN. Mr. Chairman, could I just say I had the opportunity of being with President Begaye when all this transpired. I thank him for his leadership, I thank him for his rapid response to the people of the Navajo Nation and I thank you for your very strong statement today.

I note that you are accompanied by your outstanding attorney general as well.

Thank you, Mr. Chairman.

The CHAIRMAN. Thank you, Senator McCain.

Next we will hear from the Honorable James "Mike" Olguin.

STATEMENT OF HON. JAMES "MIKE" OLGUIN, TRIBAL COUNCIL MEMBER, SOUTHERN UTE INDIAN TRIBE

Mr. OLGUIN. Good afternoon, Chairman Barrasso and Committee members.

My name is Mike Olguin. I am honored to be here. I am an elected member of the Southern Ute Tribal Council which is the governing body of the Southern Ute Indian Tribe. Thank you for the opportunity to appear before you today on behalf of the tribe and to discuss the Gold King Mine spill and its impact on the tribe and our community.

At this time, Mr. Chairman, I would like to mention a few items from my written statement and then answer any questions you or the Committee members may have.

The Animas River crosses the tribe's reservation downstream of Durango, Colorado and upstream of New Mexico. Since the Gold King Mine blew out on August 5, the tribe has been extensively engaged in responding to the spill.

We first learned of the Gold King Mine release when the Colorado Department of Natural Resources notified the tribe on the afternoon of the spill. We immediately responded by implementing our emergency management plan, contacting the county office of emergency management, EPA and sampling water quality before the spill reached the reservation.

In the first days after the spill, it was largely the local jurisdictions who responded to the incident. The tribe issued a disaster declaration on Saturday, August 8th. Other jurisdictions followed suit.

In the days following the release, we attended to the needs of the tribal membership. We posted signs closing access to the river on the reservation, delivered bottled water, provided water tanks and water for livestock, held informational meetings with tribal members and offered temporary housing for affected tribal members. Additionally, we coordinated EPA testing of tribal member domestic water wells.

For the duration of the response, tribal staff actively participated with personnel from other affected governments in the Unified Incident Command and remains engaged in the Incident Command to this day.

As of Friday after the spill, the EPA still did not have a coordinated effort in Durango. In the absence of a Federal presence, local jurisdictions, including the tribe, worked together. For example, on August 6, the tribe's water quality program called New Mexico's Spill Reporting Hotline and reported the spill to New Mexico. At that point, neither EPA nor Colorado had notified New Mexico.

The county and our tribe notified our sister tribe, the Ute Mountain Ute Tribe, of the spill. We also shared information with downstream tribes in the lower Colorado River Basin.

For the period from August 5th through September 8th, the tribe has incurred approximately $170,000 in costs in responding to the spill, mostly in staff time. We understand neighboring community businesses suffered losses and our neighboring local governments also incurred costs. We are working with EPA to obtain reimbursement for costs already expended and future costs that will be incurred, including the cost of continued water quality monitoring.

The tribe has had a long, active water sampling program funded by EPA's Tribal Assistance Program Clean Water Act grants. The tribe's water quality data provided valuable information to all the parties affected by the Gold King Mine spill.

We tested before the plume hit the reservation and for two weeks after the spill. During that time, we were testing daily for over 25 substances, including aluminum, silver, magnesium, arsenic, lead and mercury.

Coincidentally, just two weeks before the Gold King spill, we had collected tissue samples from fish in the Animas to conduct metal analysis of those samples. We shared our water quality data and continued monitoring should provide important information on the long term impacts.

Like others, we favor a full evaluation of events leading to the spill and EPA's performance in responding to the spill. However, it is important to keep this incident in perspective and understand it points to a much larger problem.

There are estimated to be 20,000 abandoned mines in Colorado alone causing water pollution problems. Federal leadership, assistance and cooperation among downstream community stakeholders is key to avoiding another blowout and addressing the problem of abandoned mine drainage polluting the Upper Animas River Watershed.

Thank you for the opportunity to appear before you today.

[The prepared statement of Mr. Olguin follows:]

PREPARED STATEMENT OF HON. JAMES "MIKE" OLGUIN, TRIBAL COUNCIL MEMBER, SOUTHERN UTE INDIAN TRIBE

Good afternoon Chairman Barrasso, Vice Chairman Tester, and Committee members. Thank you for the opportunity to appear before you today on behalf of the Southern Ute Indian Tribe to discuss the Gold King Mine Spill and its impacts on the Tribe and our community.

My name is Mike Olguin. I am an elected member of the Southern Ute Indian Tribal Council, which is the governing body of the Southern Ute Indian Tribe. The Southern Ute Indian Reservation encompasses approximately 710,000 acres in southwestern Colorado. The Tribe is blessed by eight rivers traversing its Reservation in five main drainage basins. One of those rivers is the Animas River, which bisects the western half of the Tribe's Reservation, downstream of Durango, Colorado, and upstream of New Mexico.

Since the Gold King Mine blowout on August 5, the Tribe has been actively and extensively engaged in responding to the spill. Because of this experience, the Tribe has learned some lessons and is prepared to share our observations with the Committee.

Tribal and Local Governments Were Particularly Responsive and EPA was Cooperative in Responding to the Spill

The Tribe first learned of the Gold King Mine release when the Deputy Director of the Colorado Department of Natural Resources notified the Tribe's Wildlife Resources Division on Wednesday afternoon, August 5, 2015. Our Tribe immediately responded by implementing its emergency management plan, contacting the La Plata County Office of Emergency Management, estimating when the contaminant plume would reach the Reservation, contacting EPA to determine the appropriate analyte list for water quality sampling, and commencing baseline water quality monitoring activities before the spill reached the Reservation. On Thursday and Friday, August 6th and 7th, tribal staff coordinated with EPA and La Plata County personnel, attended meetings, gathered information, and continued daily sampling on the Animas River. In the first days of the spill, however, it was largely the local jurisdictions who were responding to the incident. As of Friday, August 7th, EPA still did not have a coordinated effort in Durango. In the absence of a federal presence, local jurisdictions, including the Tribe, worked together as members of the Southwest Incident Management Team in coordinating a response.

In accordance with the Tribe's Incident Management Plan, Tribal Chairman Clement Frost issued a disaster declaration on Saturday, August 8th. Other jurisdictions followed suit. In the days that followed the release, the Tribe attended to the needs of the tribal membership. The Tribe posted signs closing access to the Animas River on the Reservation, commenced bottled water delivery to affected tribal members, provided water tanks for affected livestock owners, commenced delivery of water for livestock (the Tribe commenced delivering water to the tribal membership when the EPA contractor delivered water that was not suitable for livestock consumption), held informational meetings with tribal members, and offered temporary housing for affected tribal member families. The Tribe also coordinated and supported EPA testing of tribal member domestic water wells and irrigation ditches in the impacted area within the Reservation. Subsequently, the Tribe purchased and installed 14 reverse osmosis systems on the kitchen taps of tribal member homes.

For the duration of the response, tribal staff communicated, coordinated, and actively participated with personnel from other affected governments in the Unified Incident Command. The Tribe's Incident Management Team was fully engaged in the Incident Command effort, which was headquartered in Durango, and worked closely with local, state and federal agencies throughout the response effort. Tribal Incident Management Team members staffed the center virtually around the clock to ensure that the Tribe was contributing its expertise to the response effort, as well as to ensure that the Tribe was treated as an affected jurisdiction. The Tribe has since received acknowledgement and thanks for its participation, expertise, efficacy, and professionalism in responding to the incident, and remains engaged in the Incident Command to this day.

The spill response highlighted the importance of relationships between state, tribal, and local governments. The State of New Mexico first learned of the spill on August 6th when the Southern Ute Indian Tribe's Water Quality Program called New Mexico's Spill Reporting Hotline. New Mexico had not received notification from either EPA or Colorado at that point. The County and City attorneys reached out to tribal attorneys to share information and meeting notifications that they knew had not been shared with tribal attorneys. The Southern Ute Indian Tribe coordinated with its sister tribe, the Ute Mountain Ute Tribe, which draws water from the San Juan River. Other downstream tribes in the lower Colorado River Basin, including Chemehuevi, Fort Mohave, Quechan, and Cocopah reached out to the Southern Ute Indian Tribe for information about the spill and the Tribe's water quality sampling, which the Southern Ute Indian Tribe shared.

Today, water quality monitoring results show the water of the Animas River on the Reservation has returned to pre-spill conditions and the River has been reopened for all activities. Our primary concern remains the potential long-term impact on human health and the environment caused by the deposition of heavy metals on the Animas Riverbed.

The Tribe Incurred Significant Costs from Responding to the Spill but Expects Full Reimbursement from EPA

For the period from August 5th through September 8th, the Tribe incurred approximately $170,000 in costs responding to the spill, mostly in staff time. We understand neighboring community businesspersons suffered losses and our neighboring local governments, La Plata County and the City of Durango, with whom the Tribe shares many interests, likewise incurred costs. Long-term, we expect to incur costs for continued water quality and sediment monitoring. The Tribe is working with EPA to enter into a Cooperative Agreement whereby the EPA will reimburse the Tribe for costs already expended, as well as future costs that will be incurred, including the costs of continued water quality monitoring.

The Tribe's Water Quality Data Provided Important Information for Assessing the Spill's Short-term Impacts and Continued Monitoring Should Provide Important Information on Long-term Impacts

The Tribe has long had an active water sampling and monitoring program, and for over fifteen years has been monitoring water quality in the rivers that cross the Reservation, including the Animas. Before the Gold King Spill, the Tribe's Water Quality Program had been maintaining three stations in the River with equipment that continuously collects pH, oxygen, temperature, and conductivity data. EPA funds this monitoring through a Clean Water Act tribal assistance grant. In response to the spill, the Tribe's Water Quality Program established additional monitoring stations and expanded the list of substances for which the Tribe tests. The Tribe tested before the plume hit the Reservation, and for two weeks after the spill, the Tribe was testing daily for over 25 substances, including aluminum, iron, silver, magnesium, arsenic, cadmium, selenium, zinc, lead, mercury, barium, and molybdenum. The Tribe has since resumed its routine monthly sampling of water quality, quarterly sampling of macroinvertebrates, and taking pH, oxygen, temperature, and conductivity readings every 30 minutes.

On Thursday, August 13, 2015, the Tribe shared the water quality data it had collected on the Animas River since the spill. The data from the lab was encouraging. The Tribe assessed the results against tribal and state water quality standards, as well as historical data. Initial pH data showed no dip below pH 7.4 on the Reservation. Aquatic life prefers waters in the 6.5–8.0 range. The Tribe shared data with EPA, the State of Colorado, La Plata County, local officials, and community stakeholder groups. The Tribe also prepared and shared historical water quality data to provide information on pre-release—or normal—river conditions.

The Tribe also has historical data regarding aquatic life in the River. Coincidentally, just two weeks before the Gold King spill, the Tribe had collected tissue samples from fish in the Animas River to conduct metals analysis on those samples. While the purpose of the testing was initially to assess potential human consumption concerns, the Tribe will continue to conduct these fish tissue studies to determine any toxicity impacts from the spill. This will allow the Tribe to assess the extent of bioaccumulation of toxins in the aquatic life in the River.

The Tribe has been able to develop a highly successful water quality program, which has provided valuable support to the community in this response, due principally to EPA Tribal Assistance Program grant funding. We hope Congress and the EPA will see the benefits that the Tribal Assistance Program grants have provided to Indian Country and its surrounding communities and continue to appropriately fund these tribal grant programs.

The Problem of Abandoned Mine Drainage Predates the Gold King Incident, and Addressing the Problem is Complex and Expensive

Like others, the Tribe favors a full evaluation of events leading to the spill and the EPA's performance responding to the spill. We can all learn from mistakes made and, based on a thorough evaluation of the incident and response, hopefully, EPA, the Tribe, and other responders can improve emergency response preparedness.

It is important to keep this incident in perspective and understand it points to a much larger problem, one that has been 100 years in the making. In the late 19th century, the discovery of valuable minerals in the San Juan Mountains led to widespread trespass on lands set apart for the Utes under an 1868 treaty. As a result, the United States negotiated another agreement with the Utes in 1873 that carved 3.7 million acres out of the middle of the Ute Reservation. That agreement, along with the 1872 mining law, paved the way for hard rock mining in the San Juan Mountains, one legacy of which is mining-related pollution of the Animas River.

The Gold King is not the only abandoned mine polluting the Animas River basin. There are many others, and reportedly many thousands of abandoned mines that similarly degrade water quality in rivers across the West. There are an estimated 23,000 abandoned mines in Colorado alone. We hope that the new light being shined on the long-standing problem of acid mine drainage in the Animas River basin will cause interested parties to develop a permanent solution.

Federal Leadership and Assistance, and Communication, Collaboration, and Cooperation among Downstream Community Stakeholders and Federal, State, and Tribal Governments, is Key to Avoiding another Blowout and Addressing the Problem of Abandoned Mine Drainage Polluting the Upper Animas River Watershed

Without Congressional support and federal leadership, the problem of acid mine drainage polluting the Animas River and other rivers will not be solved. The Tribe, State of Colorado, local governments, and stakeholders need federal assistance in exploring options for cleaning up the acid mine drainage problem, including possible Superfund designation for the San Juan Mountain area surrounding the Gold King Mine. The Tribe urges the Committee to support continued dialogue and collaboration and to provide direction in how the Tribe and other interested parties can help EPA respond to contamination threats, in order that EPA may fulfill its mission to protect, preserve and, where necessary, proactively remediate contamination sites that continue to threaten the Animas and other rivers.

Conclusion

The Tribe, through its Incident Management Team and Water Quality Program has made a significant contribution to the response effort on the Gold King incident. Based on ongoing discussions, we anticipate EPA will reimburse the Tribe for its direct costs incurred responding to the spill. The Tribe hopes Congress will fund, and EPA will assist in providing support for, long-term monitoring for impacts caused by the Gold King Mine spill. We also hope Congress will support EPA continuing to work cooperatively with Colorado and affected tribes, local governments, and community stakeholders to develop a permanent solution to the acid mine drainage problem in southwestern Colorado.

Thank you for the opportunity to appear before you today. I am glad to answer questions the Committee may have.

The CHAIRMAN. Thank you very much and we appreciate your testimony.

Mr. Douglas Holtz-Eakin.

STATEMENT OF DOUGLAS HOLTZ–EAKIN, PRESIDENT, AMERICAN ACTION FORUM

Mr. HOLTZ-EAKIN. Chairman Barrasso, Senator Udall, Senator McCain, thank you for the privilege of being here today.

The Gold King Mine blowout is a clear environmental disaster. My goal is to shed some light on the larger economic fallout of the events.

To do that, the first step is to actually get some sense of the scale of the environmental exposure. As has been widely discussed, the initial discharge was 3 million gallons, although there are reports of continued discharge at a relatively high rate of 610 gallons per minute.

If one extrapolates that from the moment of the blowout to this hearing, there is an additional 37 million gallons of discharge into the watershed.

The second step is to put some economic value on this discharge. The conventional way to do that is to add up the direct costs, alternative water supplies, hay, cleanup costs, add to that loss economic activity like empty hotel rooms and cancelled rafting trips and the spillover into the economic livelihood in the area.

The data really were not sufficient to do that for purposes of this hearing. I still think that would be a valuable exercise.

As an alternative, we chose to turn to the EPA itself as a source for the valuation of these toxic discharges. In particular, they issued a rule for restricting the discharge of a similar class of toxins from steam-powered electric utilities. As part of that rulemaking, they identified the value of minimizing these discharges and that looks like essentially 90 cents per gallon of discharge.

If you take that number at face value, it says at the lower bound, the 3 million gallon immediate discharge, is a $2.7 million damage to the area. At the upper bound, it is a $36 million damage to the area.

In doing so, I would emphasize that the EPA's analysis is for sort of a study diminished discharge. It does not take into account the acute environmental impact of the spike in toxins, so it is probably a lower bound estimate of the kind of impacts you would get.

In terms of perspective, it is also worth thinking about the fact that about 500 other such abandoned mine possibilities in the area. If we were to replicate the same series of disastrous steps, that is about a $1.35 trillion economic exposure.

I would emphasize that there is an enormous amount of economic activity at risk and impacts to the region. As you well know, the watershed covers four States and many key rivers, the Animas, the San Juan and also Lake Powell but in particular, it affects the tribes whose representatives sit next to me.

I think it is important to recognize these are populations not well situated to take that large an economic hit. As emphasized in the hearing already, poverty and unemployment rates hover above 40 percent in some cases and these are economic institutions that rely heavily on water and have large amounts of agriculture.

The Navajo Nation has about $40 million a year in production and $2.5 million in exports. Bearing the cost of these kinds of impacts is a severe hardship for the tribes. I think it should be a priority to make sure that those costs are minimized as much as possible.

In closing, I would emphasize two more things about that. First, it is obvious that the dry economic dollar should not capture the damages to cultural values and the kinds of things President Begaye talked about. You should look at all of this as sort of a lower bound on the impact the tribes will bear.

The second is, from an economics point of view, it is not the actual damages and the actual duration of the environmental damage that matters. It is the perceived damage. If I am going to buy the export of Navajo cherries, as a customer what I care about is the perception that they might still be tainted by the discharge from the Gold King Mine.

In that regard, clarity in the actual environmental damages and clarity in the health risks consumers of those products and producers of those products face is not just something which is I think a standard of good government-to-government relations, it is an imperative for repairing the economic damage of this blowout, to restore the confidence in the products these tribes produce.

I thank you for the chance to be here today.

[The prepared statement of Mr. Holtz-Eakin follows:]

PREPARED STATEMENT OF DOUGLAS HOLTZ-EAKIN, PRESIDENT, AMERICAN ACTION FORUM*

Chairman Barrasso, Vice Chairman Tester and Members of the Committee, thank you for the opportunity to appear today to discuss the impacts of the Environmental Protection Agency's (EPA's) Gold King Mine disaster. In today's testimony I wish to make three main points:

- Although there is no direct precedent for the toxic Animas River spill in Colorado, past EPA estimates indicate that the spill could cost between $338 million and $27.7 billion;
- If each of the 500,000 known Abandoned Mine Lands (AMLs) released as much toxic waste into the rivers as the Gold King mine, the total would amount to 1.5 trillion gallons. Using the same method for estimating the lower-bound cost of the Gold King mine spill, the 500,000 AMLs would cost an estimated $1.35 trillion dollars; and
- Transparency within the Environmental Protection Agency remains elusive. The Gold King case shows inaction, poor planning and misleading statements by top officials. Prevention planning and mitigation were not adequately executed.

Let me provide some background on the spill as well as detail to each of these points.

Gold King Mine Blowout

Ironically, in an attempt to prevent contaminating water, a team under the supervision of the EPA was the catalyst that caused over 3 million gallons of toxic waste to be released into the Animas River on August 5th, 2015.[1] These toxins included neurotoxins, lead arsenic, thallium and other heavy metals from the abandoned Gold King mine. The contracted company, Environmental Restoration LLC underestimated the built-up volume of water, and in an attempt to install a pump to draw out the water triggered the breach.[2] The polluted water, which has covered 300 miles to date, entered the Animas and San Juan rivers through Cement Creek and has now reached Lake Powell in Utah.[3]

The spill prompted emergencies in three states as well as two American Indian tribes, the Navajo and the Ute, which will bear the brunt of both the direct and indirect costs. Some of those costs are already apparent, while others will come to light months or even years from now. The toxins caused the wastewater coming

*I thank Kim Van Wyhe and Jacqueline Varas for their assistance. All opinions expressed herein are my own and do not represent the position of the American Action Forum.

from the Gold King Mine to turn a mustard yellow color created by high acidity and iron bound to solid particles (see picture). [4] The abandoned mine was closed in 1923 and is currently owned by Todd Hennis, President of San Juan Corp. [5]

Source: IFL Science

Tribal Impacts

The spill, which has been identified as one of the worst hard rock mining related disasters in decades has been detrimental to its surrounding community. Local business centered around the river has dried up, farming has come to a halt and the sheer public safety threat that the 3 million plus gallons of toxic mining waste created has left waterways in Colorado, Utah, New Mexico and Arizona in peril. Studies suggest it will take decades to restore the affected waterways and surrounding areas. [6]

The Navajo Nation is the largest Indian reservation in the United States with approximately 300,000 residents spread across 27,000 square miles. [7] After the San Juan River was contaminated with toxic heavy metals from Gold King Mine, Navajo leaders were forced to close the river for more than three weeks. [8] This left the reservation's agricultural economy in significant danger, as the Navajo Nation's 30,000 acres of crops depend on river water for survival. [9] The polluted wastewater negatively impacted over 215 miles of farmland as well native populations of fish, wildlife, and livestock. [10] The spill took an additional toll on Navajo Nation residents, who utilize the river daily for cooking, cleaning, and bathing. The Navajo Nation declared a state of emergency on August 11, but both the Federal Emergency Management Agency (FEMA) and the EPA have rejected the tribe's requests for federal aid. [11]

According to the Navajo Nation's Division of Natural Resources ''Water is Life,'' and ''Without water, farming and raising livestock would not be possible''. [12] Throughout the Navajo Nation, many communities were established and grew because of the water available to them. The Colorado River and San Juan River are some of the major waterways that go through Navajo Nation and Lake Powell, although not on Navajo land has more than 2,000 miles of southern shoreline located on the Navajo Nation. [13]

Agriculture is the largest private-sector employer on the Navajo Nation. Navajo agriculture exports average $2.5 million dollars per year producing staples of pinto beans, corn, wheat and fresh produce such as apricots and cherries, total production comes out to around $37.5 million per year. [14] The tribes rely heavily on the San Juan River for both irrigation and for livestock needs to support this growing industry.

For the past 42 days, $892,000 in revenue has been potentially lost, as the Navajo tribe has been unable to depend on the rivers due to the toxic waste. If this situation is not resolved soon, the Navajo's agriculture industry could be crippled. Using the lost days and total production. The Navajo nation has the potential to lose $1.25 million dollars per month or $41,000 dollars a day. A little over two weeks ago, Navajo Nation president Russell Begaye met with farmers to discuss plans to reopen the irrigation canal near the town of Shiprock, however due to the environmental degradation and safety hazards that are associated with the river the farmers overruled Begaye and voted 104–0 to maintain existing closures for a year. [15]

The Southern Ute Indian tribe was the first to see toxic waste invade its waters, as the Animas River runs directly through its reservation. The reservation covers 1,059 square miles in 3 counties and is comprised of the oldest residents of Colorado. [16] The Southern Ute Indians, like the Navajos, declared a state of local disaster after determining that the resources needed to manage the spill exceeded the tribe's capabilities. Much like the Navajo Nation, the Southern Ute Tribe is dependent on river water for fishing, farming, and the preservation of its natural resources. Although the long-term effects of the spill on wildlife are not yet known, the EPA's actions and subsequent closure of the Animas River has been detrimental to the tribe's quality of life and local economy.[17] The Ute Mountain Ute reservation was also affected by the spill citing that portions of their 8,500 acre reservation were also affected by the Gold King blowout.

In an independent assessment conducted by the Southern Ute Tribe it was noted that total response effort expenses that were incurred due to the spill have reached over $200,000 which has added a 45 percent burden to employee straight time. This number does not include the economic loss that has and will occurred as a result of the spill.

Estimating the Costs of the Animas River spill

Only time will reveal the full direct and indirect costs associated with this massive spill. The lost income, and impact on tribal living are yet to be seen but representatives from the Navajo Nation have said that the river is "an economic base that sustains the people that live along the river".[18]

The American Action Forum (AAF) recently analyzed EPA data in a study entitled "What will EPA's Toxic Animas River Spill Cost?" to determine the costs of toxic waste in the due to the Gold King Mine blowout. The study found that a new EPA regulation, which aims to limit the "amount of toxic metals and other pollutants discharged to surface waters" by steam electric power plants, attributes $424 million of annual benefits for reducing 0.47 billion pounds of toxic discharge. Therefore, an approximate estimate for the benefit of avoiding toxic waste was found to be 90 cents per gallon ($424 million/470 million gallons).[19]

When this estimate is applied to the Gold King Mine spill, the cost of the 3 million gallons of toxic wastewater spilled from the mine is estimated to be around $2.7 million. However, the costs may be much higher. At last week's hearing before the House Science, Space and Technology Committee,[20] Dr. Benn the Executive Director for the Navajo Nation Environmental Protection Agency stated that the chemical spill from the Gold King Mine continues to flow at a rate of 610 gallons per minute.[21] The spill was said to have occurred at 10:58 am Mountain Time Zone. Using the time of the occurrence as well as the estimated the flow rate, AAF determined that since the initial spill, 37,012,970 additional gallons of toxic waste have been flowing (as of the start of this hearing at 2:15 pm today). The additional 37 million barrels brings the price tag to just over $36 million dollars and counting.

The EPA's power plant rule also serves as a useful guide for estimating the costs of the Gold King Mine spill because it refers to the prevention of arsenic and lead, toxic metals that were among those toxins released into the Animas River. However, the EPA's estimates represent the benefits of avoiding gradual water pollution, not acute environmental disasters. Also, they do not take into account direct costs that were imposed on residents in surrounding areas, which resulted from their inability to access the river for farming, fishing, recreation, and tourism. When these factors are taken into account, the total costs of the EPA's river water pollution may be significantly higher.[22]

It should be noted that the EPA's affluent discharge rule was not designed to regulate acute pollution events, but rather the gradual effects of water pollution. For example, the Animas River had 300 to 3,500 times the normal levels of arsenic and lead. In addition, the figure of $2.7 million probably does not account for the value of "non-use" benefits that EPA and the Department of the Interior (DOI) attempted to quantify in the past. Here, there are direct use costs because thousands of local residents, farmers, anglers, and tourists cannot use the river in its polluted state.

Abandoned Mine Lands

There are over 500,000 abandoned mines like that of the Gold King Mine in the United States. These abandoned mine lands or AML's pose a serious threat to human health and the environment according to the Abandoned Land Mine Portal. Environmental degradation, including sedimentary and sediment contamination, water pollution, air pollution, threats to wildlife and endangered species and public safety concerns are just a few of the dangers associated with AML's.[23] If each of the 500,000 mines released as much toxic waste into the rivers as the Gold King mine, the total would be around 1.5 trillion gallons. Using the same method for estimating the cost of the Gold King mine spill (at the lower-bound figure of $2.7 million) the 500,000 AML's would cost the American taxpayer an estimated $1.35 trillion dollars. The map below shows the state of Colorado's reclamation projects and includes the state's abandoned mines and mines under remediation.[24]

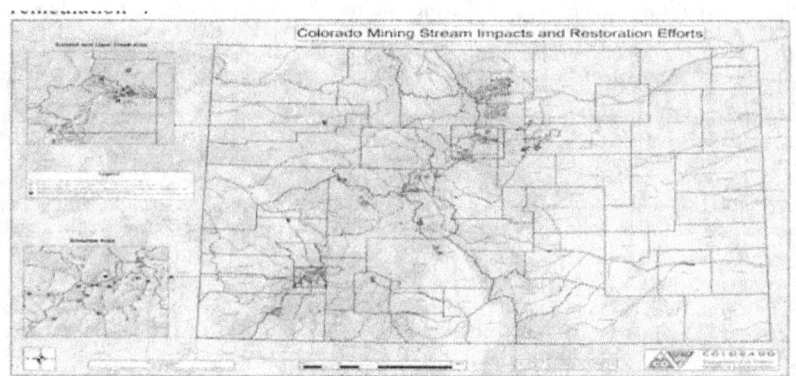

Source: *Colorado Public Radio*

According to the Bureau of Land Management (BLM), the AML program (which is run under the Department of the Interior's Office of Surface Management) has a current funding request for $28.7 million dollars. [25] This is an increase of $1.3 million from last year. BLM states that "The Surface Mining Control and Reclamation Act established the Abandoned Mine Reclamation Fund to receive the Abandoned Mine Land fees and finance reclamation of coal AML sites. The increase includes $700,000 for applied science studies pertaining to abandoned mines and $291,000 for project monitoring. Based on this funding it would take DOI over 143 plus years to pay for the cleanup of the 500,000 mines.

In 2009, the BLM released a study entitled "Feasibility Study for AML Inventory Validation and Physical Safety Closures" [26] that determined the total cost to complete field validation and physical safety remediation at 22,104 AML physical safety sites came out to $402.6 million. BLM concluded that of that $402.6 million, $11.4 million would be required to field validate and remediate all high-priority sites impacting public safety and that $12.6 million would be required to field validate and remediate the medium priority sites and an additional $377.7 million would be needed to field validate and remediate sites that are characterized as low priority. This price tag to ensure physical and environmental safety is miniscule in comparison to the cleanup and remediation efforts that would be needed if more of these spills were to occur.

EPA Transparency

In 2014, the EPA was warned that that there was a serious risk of a blowout at the Gold King mine. This raises the question as to why the EPA wasn't prepared for such an incident and didn't have proper containment procedures in place? According to a 92-page document that was released by the EPA "Conditions may exist that could result in a blow-out of the blockages and cause a release of large volumes of contaminated mine waters and sediment from inside the mine, which contain concentrated heavy metals. [27]" Despite the explicit warning the EPA did nothing to mitigate the problem. In fact, no remediation work or maintenance had been done on Gold King mine in almost a quarter of a century. The aforementioned documents did not include any details of the spill and many of the 92 pages were redacted leading to questions regarding to transparency within the agency, reports cite that much of the redacted information came from the 2013 safety plan. It was also revealed that it took the EPA nearly a day to inform local officials of the incident; for 24 hours there were people and businesses relying on this water source without any knowledge of the toxins that were running rampant.

EPA Chief Gina McCarthy declared a moratorium on all mine remediation across the country until it can be concluded how the Gold King spill occurred. [28] McCarthy said the EPA will take time to "properly review and analyze the data" which is leaving the surrounding communities waiting for answers.

Conclusion

The Gold King Mine spill will cost a significant amount to clean up, and an unknown additional amount to monitor residual effects from the toxins. These factors will make the indirect costs as a result of the spill also indefinite for quite some time. Communities are in danger and the tribes who depend on these rivers have to find alternate water sources or relocate in order to survive.

Had the EPA taken the proper precautions and heeded their own warnings, this situation could have been avoided. The avoidance and lack of preparation for abandoned mine lands in the United States is quite evident, and potentially quite costly. It would be prudent of the EPA and DOI to come up with a plan in order to not be in the same position again and impose on the American taxpayer the costs of another careless mistake.

Thank you for your time and I am happy to answer any questions you may have.

Sources

[1] *http://www2.epa.gov/goldkingmine*

[2] *https://www.cpr.org/news/story/gold-king-mine-1887-claim-private-profits-and-social-costs*

[3] *http://www.huffingtonpost.com/entry/epa-knew-of-risk-for-toxic-spill\55d8f1afe4b0a40aa3ab32e3*

[4] *http://www.iflscience.com/environment/canary-gold-king-mine-legacy-abandoned-mines-means-more-spills*

[5] *http://www.cpr.org/news/story/gold-king-mine-1887-claim-private-profits-and-social-costs*

[6] *http://www.theguardian.com/us-news/2015/aug/10/colorado-spill-animas-river-durango-toxic-orange*

[7] *http://www.discovernavajo.com/fact-sheet.aspx*

[8] *http://www.denverpost.com/news/ci\28720782/navajo-nation-reopens-irrigation-canal-3-weeks-after*

[9] *http://gazette.com/navajo-nation-says-it-feels-brunt-of-colorado-mine-leak/article/1557261*

[10] *http://www.marketplace.org/topics/sustainability/navajo-nation-among-those-affected-mine-disaster*

[11] *http://www.kob.com/article/stories/s3898844.shtml#.Ve9BU\RSJ2w*

[12] *http://dnrnavajo.org/*

[13] *http://dnrnavajo.org/*

[14] *http://www.progressive-economy.org/trade\facts/navajo-farm-exports-2–3-million-per-year/*

[15] *http://www.theguardian.com/environment/2015/aug/26/gold-king-mine-spill-navajo-nation-farmers-animas-river-water*

[16] *https://www.southernute-nsn.gov/*

[17] http://indiancountrytodaymedianetwork.com/2015/08/13/southern-ute-tribe-declares-disaster-over-mining-spill-animas-river-161377

[18] *http://nypost.com/2015/08/12/navajo-nation-feels-brunt-of-colorado-mine-leak/*

[19] *http://americanactionforum.org/insights/what-will-epas-toxic-animus-river-spill-cost*

[20] *https://science.house.gov/sites/republicans.science.house.gov/files/documents/HHRG-114-SY-WState-DBenn-20150909.pdf*

[21] *http://www.usgs.gov/blogs/features/usgs\top\story/understanding-the-effects-of-abandoned-mine-lands-on-the-environment/*

[22] *http://americanactionforum.org/insights/what-will-epas-toxic-animus-river-spill-cost*

[23] *http://www.abandonedmines.gov/*

[24] *https://www.cpr.org/news/story/gold-king-mine-1887-claim-private-profits-and-social-costs*

[25] *http://www.osmre.gov/*

[26] *http://www.blm.gov/style/medialib/blm/wo/MINERALS\REALTY\AND\RESOURCE\PROTECTION—/aml/aml\documents.Par.86129.File.dat/AML%20FeasibilityStudy\PSH.pdf*

[27] *http://www2.epa.gov/region8/upper-animas-mining-district*

[28] *http://www.popsci.com/secret-history-epas-animas-river-spill*

The CHAIRMAN. Thank you very much.

Dr. David Weindorf.

STATEMENT OF DAVID C. WEINDORF, ASSOCIATE DEAN FOR RESEARCH, COLLEGE OF AGRICULTURAL SCIENCES AND NATURAL RESOURCES, TEXAS TECH UNIVERSITY

Mr. WEINDORF. Chairman Barrasso, Senators McCain and Udall, thank you kindly for the opportunity to testify before you this afternoon.

My name is Dr. David C. Weindorf. I serve as Associate Dean for Research in the College of Agricultural Sciences and Natural Resources at Texas Tech University.

Approximately two weeks after the Gold Mine Spill, I was contacted by Rick Strait, New Mexico State Soil Scientist for the USDA Natural Resources Conservation Service. He urgently requested my help in assessing soil quality in and along the Animal River Watershed in northwestern New Mexico.

Quickly, a partnership was forged between the NRCS, New Mexico State University, who operates a field research station in Farmington, New Mexico, represented today by Dr. Kevin Lombard here with us, as well as myself of Texas Tech University, a soil scientist with expertise in advance soil spectroscopy techniques.

From September 1 through 3, Dr. Lombard and I used a portable x-ray fluorescent spectrometer, hereafter referred to as a PXRF, to make elemental analysis of the reddish orange sludge released as part of the spill.

We also revaluated farm fields irrigated by the water taken from the Animas River, as well non-irrigated soils in the valley which we scanned as control samples. In all, we scanned 140 samples in three days.

The PXRF spectrometer measures around 20 different elements on-site in 60 seconds with parts per million accuracy and is backed by reference methods set forth by the NRCS, Soil Science Society of America, EPA and several European agencies.

My scanning extended from the farms on the Navajo Nation up through the farming communities of Farmington and Aztec, north into Colorado and ended just north of Durango, Colorado where remnant sludge from the spill was still widely present all over the river shorelines as you will see in photo 1.

Even though the large initial pollutant plume has now passed and the water has once again become clear, in parts of the river, large amounts of the contaminant sludge remains. I call your attention to the photo where you clearly see the river flowing clearly but it is bordered by the deposition of reddish orange sludge along the river banks and in the sediment along the bottom of the river.

Using the PXRF spectrometer, we determined that he lead concentration of the sludge average 637 ppm, more than ten times the background level of lead in the control soils of the area. Notably, the residential screening limit for lead concentration in soils is 400 ppm.

Similarly, the sludge displayed high levels of arsenic, zinc, copper and iron relative to control soils of the area. I am aware this disputes the conclusion previously voiced today that pre-spill levels of elements are now present along the river. Clearly, they are not.

Luckily, farmers of the Animas River Valley were quick to close off the irrigation ditches connected to the river, thus keeping the worst of the pollutant plume, that reddish, orange, cloudy water, from entering their farm fields and irrigation systems.

Now that water has once again turned clear, I am worried about an even more insidious threat that looms. With the water clear, the television cameras are gone and the farmers are starting to turn on their irrigation water once again from the Animas River.

However, the large volume of contaminated sediment found both on the river embankments and within the river channel itself, as you see in photo 3, will now make its way downstream in small amounts, a sort of death by paper cuts, if you will.

Hydrologic pulses to the river caused by spring snow melt and flash floods will now wash small amounts of the pollutant into the river as suspended sediment. Photo 4 shows a kind of muddy water of the suspended sediment in the Animas River flowing through the Navajo Nation just three weeks ago while I was there.

This suspended sediment translocation can occur for years to come, posing a threat of bioaccumulation in the soils and crops irrigated by Animas River water.

The CHAIRMAN. I want to make sure we are caught up with the pictures.

Mr. WEINDORF. Yes.

The farmers have once again started to irrigate but small amounts of the metals, most of those which are positively charged cat ions, will be deposited into the soils and bind to negatively charged soil particles which will accumulate over time. You see that irrigation in my last photo.

Subject to funding approval, the NRCS, New Mexico State, Texas Tech team has already devised a plan and has that plan in place to provide long term monitoring of the farm fields in the Animas River Valley through extensive on-site PXRF scanning and monitoring the fields irrigated with Animal River water to include farms on the Navajo Nation. In fact, we have already demonstrated this PXRF technology to the Navajo Nation and EPA.

For long term assessment, we seek to work directly with local farmers who trust both NRCS conservation programs as well as New Mexico State University outreach efforts. In essence, this is local people helping local people.

Without this type of monitoring to ensure soil quality of the area, I feel the public perception of the food and fiber produced in the river valley will be harmed and the quality of the soils will be placed at risk.

We stand ready to work with local farmers of northwest New Mexico and on the Navajo Nation to ensure optimal agronomic production in the face of this environmental degradation.

Thank you again. I will be glad to take any questions you may have.

[The prepared statement of Mr. Weindorf follows:]

PREPARED STATEMENT OF DAVID C. WEINDORF, ASSOCIATE DEAN FOR RESEARCH, COLLEGE OF AGRICULTURAL SCIENCES AND NATURAL RESOURCES, TEXAS TECH UNIVERSITY

Rapid Assessment of Soil Metal Concentrations Along the Animas River, New Mexico

David C. Weindorf[1] Kevin Lombard[2]

[1]Assocaite Dean for Research & BL Allen Endowed Chair of Pedology, Department of Plant and Soil Science, Box 42122, Texas Tech University, Lubbock, TX, 79409

david.weindorf@ttu.edu

[2]Associate Professor of Horticulture, New Mexico State University Agricultural Science Center at Farmington and San Juan College Department of Science and Math, P.O. Box 1018, Farmington, NM 87499

klombard@nmsu.edu

ABSTRACT

Problem: On August 5th, 2015 an inadvertent breech at a mining facility in Colorado spilled 3 million gallons of metal laden wastewater into the Animas River. Soil Quality Assessment Team: Texas Tech University (TTU) features the largest non-land grant College of Agriculture in the United States with specialized expertise in proximal soil sensing; New Mexico State University (NMSU) is the land grant university of New Mexico with a field research station in Farmington, a town affected by the spill; US Department of Agriculture – Natural Resources Conservation Service (USDA-NRCS) is the chief agency tasked with providing American farmers and ranchers with financial and technical assistance to voluntarily implement conservation practices, enhance environmental quality, and optimize agricultural operations. Technology Utilized: Portable x-ray fluorescence spectrometry, capable of quantifying elemental concentrations in soils with parts per million accuracy on–site in 60 seconds. Key Findings: Areas of metal laden sludge showed higher levels of Fe, Cu, Zn, As, and Pb relative to natural soils of the area. The sludge itself exceeds the residential screening limits of permissible metals levels in soils. Moving Forward: While the initial large plume of sludge pollution has moved downstream, large areas of the sludge were deposited along riverbanks, fouling such areas to this day. As these materials are slowly eroded and moved downstream, concerns exist over metal accumulation in soils of the Animas River Valley where farmers use Animas River water for irrigation of their crops. Operational Plans: While other agencies are chiefly tasked with cleanup, our soil quality assessment team (TTU, NMSU, USDA-NRCS) has a plan in place to work with local farmers and provide long term monitoring of metal levels in irrigated fields from Colorado through the Navajo Nation to ensure soil quality is not degraded by use of Animas River water for crop irrigation. This plan has been submitted to the chief of USDA-NRCS for consideration and funding.

INTRODUCTION

On August 5th, 2015 an inadvertent breech of a mine shaft holding metal laden waters in Colorado was spilled into the Animas River and traversed many areas of southwest Colorado and northwest New Mexico. Farming communities in the area frequently draw irrigation water from the Animas, raising concerns that metal-laden water in the river was and/or will be spread across farm fields as irrigation water. As the plume of pollution moved down the river as a bright orange, cloudy suspension, New Mexico State University was instrumental in collecting numerous soil samples from irrigation ditches and surrounding farm fields in the vicinity of Aztec and Farmington, New Mexico prior to impact by the pollution plume. These samples will be invaluable in establishing the metal concentrations in the irrigation ditches and farmlands prior to the Gold King Mine spill.

As the pollutant plume moved down the river, a reddish orange sludge was deposited in the river sediment and along the riverbanks. Initially, river water carrying the pollutant plume was cloudy as the sludge was suspended in the water. However, after several weeks, the initial plume ran its course downstream and the water now running down the Colorado portion of the Animas River near Durango appears quite clear; so clear in fact that the coating of the reddish orange sludge on the bottom of the river and adjacent banks is readily apparent (Fig. 1). Luckily, as the initial plume of contamination was moving down the river, residents in Aztec, Farmington, and the Navajo Nation had the opportunity to shut off their irrigation ditches, preventing the most contaminated of the water from entering their fields via irrigation water. The concern now is a much more insidious one, whereby the remaining sludge in the river will slowly be carried downstream as irrigation ditches are once again activated (Fig. 2) and irrigation resumes. In this instance, the water will likely appear quite clear and useable, but the likelihood of small amounts of metals contained in the slowly-migrating sludge will have the potential to accumulate in farm fields over time. Irrigation ditches, operated by a number of cooperatives and private companies, take water from the Animas River and spread it to adjacent farms all up and down the Animas River Valley (Fig. 2). Since northwestern New Mexico receives <10 inches of annual rainfall, agronomic production would not be possible without irrigation water from the river.

In an effort to rapidly respond to the threat to soil health in the farm fields of the area, a collaboration was established between the USDA-Natural Resources Conservation Service (NRCS), New Mexico State University (NMSU), and Texas Tech University (TTU); each has specific strengths that can be utilized in addressing soil quality concerns. The NRCS is widely known and accepted as an agency that partners with farmers to optimize their soil health and agronomic production through the use of improved tillage practices, conservation structures, etc. In fact, many farmers enjoy the benefits of enrolling their land in conservation programs such as the Environmental Quality Incentives Program (EQIP). As such, farmers are fond of working with NRCS and trust their personnel given decades of faithful environmental stewardship. In the same vein, New Mexico State University has a field research station established on land leased from the Navajo Nation nearby to Farmington whereby its faculty can provide direct agronomic research and outreach efforts. Dr. Lombard lives in Aztec, farms several acres, and irrigates his property with water from the Animas River. As such, he can directly understand and sympathize with local farmer concerns as he personally faces the same concerns for his property. In partnering with Texas Tech University, NMSU and the NRCS were able to link up with a research group utilizing state of the art X-ray fluorescence spectrometry for rapid, on-site analysis of soil elemental composition. This technology will be featured in two phases of the project: 1) initial, rapid, on-site assessment of metal levels in soils of the Animas River Valley, and 2) long term monitoring whereby temporal accumulations of metals can be studied and documented as irrigation with river water once again resumes.

MATERIALS AND METHODS

Portable X-ray fluorescence (PXRF) spectrometry is a novel, yet widely accepted means of rapid elemental assessment in soils and sediments. Reference methods for the technique have been developed both by the NRCS (Soil Survey Staff, 2014) and Environmental Protection Agency (US-EPA, 2007)(Method 6200) for use in soils and sediments. Essentially, the PXRF spectrometer is a handheld unit that uses low power X-rays to eject inner shell electrons from various elements. As this occurs, outer shell electrons then cascade down to fill inner shell voids, but in doing so much relinquish energy, termed *fluorescence*. The fluorescence energy is precisely measured via an integrated silicon drift detector and used to both identify which elements are present as well as their abundance. The operational theory, optimized uses, limitations and applications are summarized by Weindorf et al. (2014). Traditional elemental soil analysis relies upon digestion with caustic acids (US-EPA 1996a, 1996b), filtration, and elemental quantification via inductively coupled plasma atomic emission spectroscopy (ICP-AES) (Soltanpour et al., 1996). Whilst the ICP-AES technique is highly accurate and will remain the analytical standard for the foreseeable future, it is laboratory-based equipment and requires extensive sample processing, consumables, etc. With regards to analytical accuracy, the PXRF reported elemental values are typically within 5-10% of the certified elemental concentrations (determined via ICP-AES), only the PXRF reported values can be obtained on-site in 60 sec. Both techniques allow for multi-elemental analysis; quite commonly ~20 elements are reported by each instrument.

For rapid analysis of elemental concentrations on-site, the NRCS-NMSU-TTU team used a Delta Premium (DP-6000) PXRF featuring a Rh X-ray tube operated at 10-40 keV with elemental quantification accomplished via integrated ultra-high resolution (<165 eV) silicon drift detector. Scanning was conducted in a proprietary software configuration known as Geochem Mode which offers elemental quantification of the following elements: V, Cr, Fe, Co, Ni, Cu, Zn, W, Hg, As, Se, Pb, Bi, Rb, U, Sr, Y, Zr, Th, Mo, Ag, Cd, Sn, Sb, Ti, Mn, Mg, Al, Si, P, S, Cl, K, and Ca. Geochem mode consists of two beams; each was set to scan for 30 sec, such that one complete sample scan took 60 sec. General limits of detection for each element are provided as Fig. 3. However, the data generated by the PXRF whilst scanning provides both the elemental quantity on an element by element basis, as well as the error term for each measurement (e.g., Pb 250 mg kg^{-1}; ±5 mg kg^{-1}). Furthermore, the location of each soil scanned was georeferenced with a handheld GPS unit to catalog the location of metals/elements detected. PXRF performance was assessed via scanning of two NIST certified soil standards whereby PXRF elemental quantity was compared to certified reference values with a recovery percentage calculated on an element by element basis.

RESULTS AND DISCUSSION

On-site PXRF scanning was undertaken Sept. 1-3, 2015. In doing so, multiple types of land were evaluated to include: irrigated lands (water taken from the Animas River), non-irrigated lands (Control), and riverbank sediment. Notably, the riverbank sediment was observed to be a mix of natural alluvial sediment and Gold King Mine sludge; the two of which had substantively different elemental signatures. In total, 140 samples were scanned in three days. Summary results are provided in Table 1.

Table 1. Elemental concentration ranges and averages for soils and sediments scanned with PXRF in the Animas River Valley in Colorado and New Mexico. All units are in mg kg^{-1}.

n	Location	Al Avg	Al Range	Fe Avg	Fe Range	Cu Avg	Cu Range	Zn Avg	Zn Range	As Avg	As Range	Pb Avg	Pb Range
29	Control	64087	25413-83540	28987	9047-50891	33	ND-94	117	25-333	7	ND-13	53	12-230
67	Irrigated	53541	7281-80325	28514	4430-45217	36	11-190	175	39-819	7	ND-13	67	5-271
35	Riverbank	37749	4219-80109	36302	5818-293194	77	ND-270	365	19-1068	11	ND-38	153	10-487
9	Riverbank-Sludge	23018	3730-38781	46356	38292-75959	127	90-176	474	273-1174	40	ND-54	637	509-899
140													

Notably, we found and identified the properties of the river sludge sent down the Animas River. Generally, it has Pb levels of ~600-800 mg kg^{-1}; and higher levels of Fe, Cu, and Zn. The residential screening limit for Pb in soils is 400 mg kg^{-1} (Brevik, 2013). These sludge materials were found both in New Mexico and Colorado, both on the stream banks and underwater (Fig. 4). Irrigated lands along the Animas River tended to have slightly higher levels of metals than non-irrigated "control" areas. It is _essential_ we monitor these areas over time as more sludge sediment washes down the river and can potentially be spread out via irrigation. PXRF was highly effective at quickly collecting elemental data with results verified both by NIST certified standards and ICP analysis. The variance of PXRF data relative to certified values is ~5-10%. Extensive river pollution was found from the Colorado/New Mexico border headed north; this sludge is highly likely to move down into New Mexico over time in response to hydrologic pulses (snow melt, flash floods, etc.).

Summarily, the level of metals found in sludge along the Animas River warrants careful observation. Certainly, cleanup of the sludge is recommended in areas where it is apparent and accessible. Nonetheless, it is highly likely that small amounts of metal will continue to work their way downstream intermixed in alluvial sediments for the next several years (Fig. 5). This poses a risk of accumulation in soils whereby Animas River water is used for irrigation. Extensive spatial and temporal sampling are recommended such that the levels of metals in soils of the Animas River Valley will be more thoroughly understood in an effort to protect and optimize soil health. If areas of accumulation are noted, phytoremediation or other remediation strategies should be undertaken to ensure that the metal laden soils do not pose a risk for metal bioaccumulation in plants or feedstocks used by humans or animals.

The NRCS, NMSU, and TTU have already submitted an extensive multi-year monitoring plan for funding consideration by the national NRCS. We stand ready to assist farmers and land owners in the region in protecting the food and fiber generated on lands of historically high agronomic value.

REFERENCES

Brevik, E.C. 2013. Soils and human health - an overview. _In:_ Brevik, E.C., Burgess, L.C. (Eds.), Soils and human health. CRC Press, Boca Raton, FL, pp. 59-82.

Soil Survey Staff. 2014. Soil survey field and laboratory methods manual. Soil Survey Investigations Report No. 51. Version 2.0. USDA-NRCS National Soil Survey Center, Lincoln, NE. Available at: http://www.nrcs.usda.gov/wps/portal/nrcs/detail/soils/research/report/?cid=nrcs142p2_053371 (verified 3 December 2013).

Soltanpour, P.N., G.W. Johnson, S.M. Workman, J.B. Jones, and R.O. Miller. 1996. Inductively coupled plasma emission spectrometry and inductively coupled plasma-mass spectrometry. _In:_ Sparks, D.L. (Ed.) Methods of soil analysis – Part 3: Chemical methods. Soil Science Society of America, Madison, WI.

US Environmental Protection Agency. 1996a. Method 3050B: Acid digestion of sediments, sludges, and soils. In SW-846 Pt 1; Office 404 of Solid and Hazardous Wastes, USEPA: Cincinnati, OH. Available at: http://www.epa.gov/osw/hazard/testmethods/sw846/pdfs/3050b.pdf (verified 26 January 2014).

US Environmental Protection Agency. 1996b. Method 3052: Microwave assisted acid digestion of siliceous and organically based matrices. _In:_ Test methods for evaluating solid waste. US Environmental Protection Agency, Washington, DC, USA. Available at: http://www.epa.gov/wastes/hazard/testmethods/sw846/pdfs/3052.pdf (verified 26 January 2014).

US Environmental Protection Agency. 2007. Method 6200: Field portable X-ray fluorescence spectrometry for the determination of elemental concentrations in soil and sediment. _In:_ Test methods for evaluating solid waste. US Environmental Protection Agency, Washington, DC, USA. Available at: http://www.epa.gov/osw/hazard/testmethods/sw846/online/6_series.htm (verified 3 December 2013).

Weindorf, D.C., N. Bakr, and Y. Zhu. 2014. Advances in portable x-Ray fluorescence (PXRF) for environmental, pedological, and agronomic applications. Advances in Agronomy 128:1-45. doi: http://dx.doi.org/10.1016/B978-0-12-802139-2.00001-9.

Fig. 1. Clear Animas River water north of Durango, Colorado showing remnants of the reddish orange colored sludge both along the river banks as well as submerged underwater.

Fig. 2. Irrigation ditches and pumps of the Animas River Valley used for spreading river water to farm fields.

Fig. 3. Generalized limits of detection for the Delta PXRF by Olympus.

Fig. 4. Assessment of sludge laden sediment with portable x-ray fluorescence spectrometry along the banks of the Animas River in New Mexico.

Fig. 5. Schematic showing how metal laden sludge along the Animas River can pose a threat to soil quality of irrigated lands in the Animas River Valley. As sediment along the riverbank washes into the river and becomes suspended, there is a high likelihood that the suspended sediments would then be dispersed across adjacent farm fields which depend on the Animas River water for irrigation.

The Gold King Mine Animas River Spill Preliminary Assessment of Surface Water, Sediments and Irrigation Ditches by Kevin Lombard and April Ulery has been retained in the Committee files.

The CHAIRMAN. Thank so much, Dr. Weindorf.
Mr. HARRISON.

STATEMENT OF GILBERT HARRISON, RANCHER AND IRRIGATOR, NAVAJO NATION

Mr. HARRISON. Yá á 'á t'ééh, Chairman Barrasso, Vice-Chairman Tester, and members of the Committee.

I am Gilbert Harrison, a member of the Navajo Tribe and work a 20 acre farm located on the Navajo Nation, a community called Gadii'ahi, along the San Juan River. Thank you for allowing me to address this important Committee.

I am 73 years old and have a wonderful wife, Gloria, an equal partner in our farming operations. I spent four years in the Marine Corps during the Vietnam conflict. I am a disabled veteran.

I have a Masters Degree and a Bachelors Degree in Electrical Engineering and am also a registered professional engineer. I worked in the aerospace industry and finished my engineering career with the Indian Health Service at the Navajo Area Office.

I was raised on a farm, except for the time I was away for education, military service and career. I am now back to farming and sheep ranching. We have a small farm growing alfalfa, hay grazer, corn, watermelon and cantaloupe.

We grow Native corn for traditional use and its pollen for Navajo ceremonies. This Navajo corn is very specific to our region and the seeds are handed down through generations.

I first heard of the Gold King Mine spill a day or two after the spill. I did not realize the magnitude of the spill until Navajo Nation President Begaye declared a state of emergency. Then I realized we had a serious water situation.

To try and save some of our crops, we hauled water from a tank provided by the BIA. USEPA provided tanks but we could not use water from these tanks because the tanks were contaminated.

Due to our age and physical abilities, we were only able to water our melons. Alfalfa, grazer and corn require lots of water, so they went without water and are damaged. It is a feeling of helplessness to watch your crops dry and die.

We will have to wait until the end of the growing season to determine our real losses, but for sure, we have lost about 40 percent of our alfalfa, 50 percent of our hay grazer, 50 percent of our corn and 20 percent on the watermelons.

Annual crop and losses are for a single year. However, alfalfa losses are long term, several years. These are cash crops and this disruption is a major setback.

I do not have crop insurance and I will have to rely solely on my claim to USEPA by a Standard Form 95. My concern is that USEPA may take a hard line and shortchange many of our claims because our farmers are not familiar with the process and are not familiar with the correct units of measure to quantify losses.

We ask Congress to urge EPA to be user friendly. After all, they have put us in this situation. Hopefully claims are processed in a timely manner.

This disastrous spill has caused social conflicts within our communities and it will take a long time to heal. The spill has caused friction between communities, between farmers and even brothers against brothers over who gets water, who does not get water and when. This is a serious issue we have not experienced before and resolving it will be very difficult.

I am very disappointed and greatly upset with the USEPA for putting us in this situation. As an engineer, I understand no matter how careful a design, Murphy's Law, if it will go wrong, it will happen. In this case, contingency plans may not have been developed. I do not feel that USEPA or its contractors were prepared for this tragic event.

We and our neighbors are now suffering the consequences. EPA should be required to design and construct safe containment and treatment systems to prevent future spills.

In closing, we are citizens of the United States. All we are asking is for fair and equal treatment to make us whole. This spill has completely disrupted our lives, economic wellbeing and social values.

Despite this awful event, we will continue to farm with the land. There is much joy in farming. With your help, we will continue to farm and irrigate from a safe water source.

Ahéhee. Thank you for providing me time to share with you our situation. I am available to answer any questions you may have.

Thank you.

[The prepared statement of Mr. Harrison follows:]

PREPARED STATEMENT OF GILBERT HARRISON, RANCHER AND IRRIGATOR, NAVAJO NATION

Yáá'át'ééh (hello) Chairman Barrasso, Vice-Chairman Tester, and Members of the Committee, my name is Gilbert Harrison. I am a member of the Navajo Nation and I have a 20 acre farm located in a community on the Navajo Reservation called Gadii'ahi, along the San Juan River. My community has been directly impacted by the spill. Gadii'ahi is part of the San Juan River Farming Project, which consists of six chapters that depend entirely on the River for irrigation needs. All of the farms in this Project are mom and pop farm plots, in that they are 2, 5, 10 and in a few instances 20 acres in size. My plight is very similar to the majority of these farms. Thank you for allowing me to speak before this Committee.

Just to give you a little background about myself, I am 73 years old. I have been married to a wonderful woman, Gloria, for over 25 years, and I have raised 4 sons. I spent 4 years in the Marine Corps during the Vietnam era. I also received my Bachelors of Science and Masters degree in Electrical Engineering from Loyola Marymount in Los Angeles, California. I am a registered Professional Engineer in the State of Arizona. After college, I remained in Los Angeles for 5 years doing Aerospace Engineering work. Thereafter, I came back to Window Rock, Arizona and worked for the Navajo Nation in their Division of Economic Development for 6 years. I then worked for Indian Health Service in Window Rock at their Navajo Area Office for another 28 years. I retired from office work in 2007 and have been farming full-time since.

I was raised on a farm and have been actively farming for 25 years. On my farm, presently, I have about 7 acres for alfalfa and the rest of the acreage are divided for corn, watermelon, cantaloupe and hay grazer. I would estimate about 50 percent of my crops go toward our personal use and 50 percent go toward sale to other Navajo ranchers. We are also sheep ranchers. We use the sheep for our own personal use. I have a small farm, so the income from my farm is too small to make a living from. I depend heavily on my retirement pay. I sell a little bit of alfalfa here and there. I also sell some Navajo traditional foods converted from corn, such as steamed corn and kneel down bread and corn pollen, which is used during Navajo traditional ceremonies. This type of corn is a Navajo traditional type of corn that comes from a specialized seed handed down from generation to generation. The remainder of my crops is for household consumption. I also share some of my crops with extended family. We use some of the alfalfa and hay grazer for our sheep, which are now at our summer camp atop the Carrizo Mountains, located about 40 miles west of Shiprock, New Mexico, an area not affected by the spill.

I first heard about the spill at the Gold King Mine from our Honorable Navajo Nation Council Delegate, Amber Crotty, about a day or two after the spill occurred. It was along the lines of "did you hear there was a spill and there's a large gold plume headed our way?" The Navajo Nation Irrigation Office shut off the irrigation water from the San Juan River around the same time. Occasionally, water also gets turned off due to maintenance or other issues. So, at that particular time, I did not realize the extent of this event and the effect it would have on my farm. However, after Navajo Nation President Russell Begaye declared a State of Emergency and put a ban on San Juan River water use, I realized we were in for some rough times. I had to get water to my crops! I started hauling water for our watermelons and cantaloupes from a tank that was provided by the Bureau of Indian Affairs. Additional water tanks were also provided by the U.S. EPA, however we had received word that those tanks were contaminated, so we did not take water from those tanks.

Alfalfa has roots that extend about 12 to 18 inches deep into the ground. As such, they require a lot of water, up to 3 irrigations between cuts and there are normally 3 cuts per season. Corn also requires frequent watering. At my age of 73, I do not have the physical capability or the equipment to provide the water necessary to keep these crops fully watered. I only had the capabilities to provide water for my watermelons and cantaloupes, so I had to leave the corn and alfalfa to suffer.

It's difficult to determine at this time what my losses are with regards to alfalfa and corn. I will have to wait until the end of this growing season, in November, to figure out the loss on my annual crops. In early spring we will be able to see the areas of no growth and where we need to replant the alfalfa. However, I roughly estimate a 40 percent loss in alfalfa at this time. Generally, alfalfa has a life span of about 6 to 7 years, and we are about 3 to 4 years into this cycle. Due to this event, we will also have to buy and replant seeds to replace the damaged alfalfa stands earlier than expected. This means plowing under the entire alfalfa stand, planting rotational crops for two years, and then finally replanting alfalfa. This is an additional economic burden in labor, equipment wear and tear, fuel, seeds and fertilizer. I also roughly estimate a 50 percent loss of my corn and a 20 percent loss of my cantaloupes and watermelons. My loss on hay grazer is maybe about 50 percent. These are all very rough estimates of losses that I did not anticipate!

I do not have many sources to go to in order to recoup my losses. My farming operation is small, so I cannot carry the expense of having any crop loss insurance. As such, it looks like I will have to rely on a claim to U.S. EPA to recoup my losses. We did receive U.S. EPA's Standard Form 95, however we have not filled it out yet. We will not know the full extent of our loss until early spring, particularly in the area of alfalfa, where losses are seen not only for this year, but for years to come. EPA needs to consider this when they review our claims. Additionally some of the native crops do not fit into a "can" unit of measure, so U.S. EPA will have to be understanding. I am hoping that when I do submit a claim to the U.S. EPA, they will make good on reimbursing me for my losses in a timely manner. I am a little worried that by the time I submit my claim, U.S. EPA may no longer be under pressure from the media or Congress. As such, they may not be as willing to reimburse me for my losses. I hope Congress and other leaders will keep checking on the U.S. EPA to prevent this from happening.

This disconcerting spill event has cause social issues that may take a long time to heal, such that it pitted farmers and communities against each other, farmer against farmer, and in some cases brother against brother. Because of the contamination, there are some communities that still do not trust the water from the San Juan River. As such, they voted to keep their water system off. There are other farmers within these communities who did not agree with that decision, which placed them at odds with each other. Then, on the other side, there are communities who voted to have their irrigation water turned back on and their waters were turned on. Unfortunately, our community of Gadii'ahi is on the tail end of the system that did not get turned on. However, after a recent vote by my community to have water restored, Gadii'ahi was able to receive minimal amounts of water directly from the San Juan River by a pump system provided by the Navajo Nation last week. After about 5 weeks, I am finally getting water to my crops. The water supply is about half of the typical amount due to the capabilities of the pump, but I take whatever water I can get.

This spill caused by the U.S. EPA created a lot of chaos, confrontation, confusion and losses among the farming community. As such, I am very disappointed and greatly upset with the U.S. EPA. As a engineer, I understand that no matter the design, you have to prepare for contingencies. I do not feel that the U.S. EPA, nor their contractor, was prepared for this tragic event. We had to suffer and still are suffering the consequences. To prevent future reoccurrence of this disaster, EPA should be required to engineer and implement a design that will contain, treat, and minimize release of toxic water at the source.

Despite this event, I will continue farming. I love farming and working the land. I expect I will be doing it until I am no longer able to. With your help, I hope that I will continue farming and irrigating from a safe and continuous water supply.

Ahéhee.' Thank you for providing me a little of your time to explain my story. I am available for any questions you may have.

The CHAIRMAN. Thank you very much.

Thanks to each and every one of you for your testimony.

I am going to start with Senator McCain.

Senator McCAIN. Mr. Harrison, thank you for your service to our Country. Thank you for a very eloquent statement that I think brings into focus the emotional stress that has been unnecessarily placed on you and all of your fellow members of the Navajo Nation.

President Begaye, because I was there, I want to thank you for your leadership and your rapid action at the time this disaster happened. I do not know of any excuse for waiting five days before calling you. I think it is disrespectful to the nation-to-nation relationship that is the foundation of our Nation.

I guess my first and maybe only question to you is, especially in light of Mr. Harrison's testimony, how would you describe the stress that your citizens of the Navajo Nation have exposed to as a result of this?

Mr. HARRISON. Thank you, Senator.

It is devastating because we are faced with tremendous amounts of miscommunication of whether things are okay, whether things are not okay and you do not know which way to turn. I think that is the biggest stress we experience because we do not know who to trust anymore. That really is a problem.

Senator McCAIN. Thank you.

Mr. BEGAYE. Thank you, Senator McCain.

It is really disheartening to stand alongside a farmer, his wife, standing out in the fields saying that we used to sing to our crops, get up early in the morning and offer prayers, thankful that we have corn, that we have hay, that we have melons, squash and pumpkin.

Now, I have seen watermelon the size of this bottle of water. I know that it is gone. They know it is gone but I see them and we still take our five gallon bucket of water and are still giving water to that watermelon because like our children, we are not going to abandon them. We will stay with them all the way until they are gone. It is a total loss for them.

Not only that but this week one community experienced three suicides. We have loss three precious souls, all because of this uncertainty that has developed, the lack of help. When you see the water buffalo that is there containing 15,000 gallons of water, when you do not see hay coming anymore, when you are being abandoned in your greatest time of need, what do you do? It causes great amounts of stress.

This week, we loss three souls down in the community that uses this river and this water. We are stressed out. Our people are stressed out.

I will say this about my Navajo Nation people. We are strong, we are resilient and we will recover. We will help each other. We just ask this Committee to walk alongside us. Come back three months from now, six months from now and have a hearing right there in our community. Have a field hearing and listen to our people. They will greatly appreciate what you have done for us today.

Thank you, Senator.

Senator MCCAIN. I thank you, Mr. President. I will discuss that possibility with the leader of our Committee who is very much committed and deeply moved by the situation and your words. We will do everything we can.

In the meantime, I say the Navajo Nation is very fortunate to have your leadership in this very difficult time.

Thank you, Mr. Chairman.

The CHAIRMAN. Thank you, Senator McCain.

Senator Udall?

Senator UDALL. Thank you, Chairman Barrasso.

Let me also echo what Senator McCain said. We very much appreciate your leadership, President Begaye. You have given a very passionate statement today on behalf of your people. You have shown to be a very forthright and excellent advocate for the Navajo people.

I also think the government-to-government relationship could have been done much better. We will stand with you to make sure it improves every day into the future as you go through and work through all these difficult issues.

In your testimony, you mentioned the Navajo people need compensation and need it now. What advice are you giving individual Navajos, President Begaye, on what they should do? I know you have given some strong advice on the Form 95 but what should they do in terms of trying to get together the information to get it to the EPA? What advice are you giving there?

Mr. BEGAYE. First of all, we are asking the EPA and this Committee to lean heavily on EPA to waive that waiver of final settlement and our people get a check from EPA for one week of hauling water and paying for hay. That will be the end of their settlement; that will end the amount of monies that EPA will pay them and that will be the end of it.

We know that this loss is going to continue, not just for a month or three months or this farming season. They told us, the EPA told us, that the cleanup will take decades. That is what they said to us verbally. Taking that to heart, our people will hurt and suffer economically from this for decades.

We are saying to them keep a close record of what you have spent already, take photos of your crops, take photos of you hauling water and keep close records of this. Go ahead and start filling out the Standard Form 95 but do not sign it.

We are asking EPA, we are asking members of this body to make sure that we are given an interim form to use, not that particular form but we need an interim form our people can use so that they are compensated for their losses this week, next week and months after. That is what we are saying to them.

We would greatly appreciate this Committee helping us put that waivered language in that form so our people will be justly compensated for all their losses.

Senator UDALL. Thank you.

You have urged the EPA to designate the upper Animas as a Superfund site. That is something I support. Can you tell us the importance this action would have to the Navajo Nation?

Mr. BEGAYE. They were told this blowout was going to happen, that it was going to happen soon and they did not take care of business and they did not address adequately.

I stood at the mouth of the mine with the worker telling me what he was doing when this spill took place, an EPA worker over 40 years working for EPA was the person working the backhoe when the spill took place. He told me the story step by step on how this all happened.

He said the other mines on the other site was about to do the same thing. We know it, EPA knows it but nothing is being done about it.

It is urgent that EPA address this and address it now because there is another disaster of this proportion ready to happen. We are saying declare it a Superfund site, deal with it, clean it up because we are the ones that will suffer in the long run.

It is astounding for me to sit here this day to hear that 330 million gallons pour out of those mines every year. Where do they go? They come onto the Navajo Nation land. We are becoming a waste dump for those contaminants and I am astounded to hear that being repeated over and over from our leaders, the EPA and no one has stopped to say where are they going.

I will say even though the 300-plus million gallons pour out every year, it is not yellow like it was when a large amount came at one time. Those need to be cleaned up and cleaned up by the EPA. They need to clean up their mess.

Thank you.

Senator UDALL. Thank you, President Begaye.

Also, Chairman Barrasso, the Chairman, the Speaker of the Navajo Council was unable to be here with us. His name is Lorenzo Bates. He asked that his testimony be submitted for the record.

The CHAIRMAN. Without objection.

I would like to follow up, President Begaye.

I hear your concerns. We talked on the phone. I spoke with you, your attorney general and other members be had met prior to this.

Can you explain the tribe's experiences with EPA and your assessment essentially of their capabilities, their competence and their attitude? Could you talk a bit about capabilities, competence and attitude?

Mr. BEGAYE. Our people are questioning all three because one, they knew about it and did not do anything about it. They could have resolved the issue before it even started, but they did not. That is one.

Today in the hearings this morning and this afternoon, we are being told they are still there on the ground helping us with water and hay. That is not true. They pulled out and are not there anymore. The tanks are not on the ground. Hay is not being delivered.

We were told just a few moments ago, the Administrator said we are delivering hay. On this past Monday, she called on a conference call, two days ago that they will continue to deliver hay until this Friday. How convenient. It has always been that.

The thing they said last week during the hearing, the Science and Technology hearing, everything that was said then, the promises that were made, have remained empty. We have not seen any movement from EPA. They have not done what they said they were going to do last week. We do not anticipate them honoring what they said today.

We will hold back. The promises are empty now. There is no movement taking place, no water is being delivered, no hay is being hauled to our communities that desperately need it.

As I said over and over, they created a culture of distrust. We can do the work ourselves. EPA needs to just give us the dollars, give us the lab we need and we will test our soil and test our waters. We have competence staff to make that happen.

The CHAIRMAN. Thank you.

Can you talk about some of the discrepancies, what we heard from the Administrator today and what you are seeing on the ground? There is a significant difference. I wanted to ask you, Mr. Olguin, a similar line in terms of something we heard from the Administrator today.

The question is, when did the EPA Administrator actually first talk to the Southern Ute Nation Chairman Clement Frost about this disaster? The Administrator testified that it was a certain date. I understand it was actually much later than that.

Mr. OLGUIN. Chairman Barrasso, my understanding is that Administrator McCarthy called the Chairman Frost this past Monday, September 14th at approximately 1:30 p.m. in the afternoon.

My understanding is the conversation was probably two to four minutes and really addressed the appreciation for us working with them but also was highlighting the initiation of the cooperative agreement for reimbursement for costs, a two to four minute conversation this past Monday.

The CHAIRMAN. In terms of your commitment, can you talk a bit about how much money the tribe has spent, without reimbursement, on measures to respond to the spill, installing water filters, bottled water to your community and different things related to that?

Mr. OLGUIN. Yes. To date, we have expended approximately $170,000. We expect that number to go up even higher as we continue to do long term monitoring. This was all on the tribe's dime. We took it upon ourselves to initiate assisting our tribal membership with delivery of water for their own consumption and of course their animals.

Even today, we installed reverse osmosis units in tribal member's homes to ensure that they do have continued safe drinking water. That may expand further into their homes for a full home system as well. The costs will still continue.

The CHAIRMAN. You did that because you thought you could not rely on the EPA or FEMA to be there for you?

Mr. OLGUIN. We have always taken the position we will take care of ourselves first and then of course seek reimbursement as a second approach. It is because those relationships cannot depend on the Federal Government to timely respond.

The CHAIRMAN. Mr. Harrison, my home State of Wyoming is a ranching State. Every day our ranchers, both on and off the Wind

River Reservation, face hardships in running their ranches. Whether it is having enough water to irrigate land to grow alfalfa or dealing with livestock disease, running a ranch is never an easy business.

The EPA does not appear to make it any easier for tribal ranches like you and others on the reservation that have been impacted by the spill. You talked about family versus family, neighbor versus neighbor.

Can you talk a bit in detail about the trauma that the Navajo Nation ranching community is experiencing right now as a result of this EPA disaster?

Mr. HARRISON. Thank you, Mr. Chairman.

That is an issue because we have communities we call chapters. Some of them are very adamant about not turning on irrigation water. In our case, we are at the very end of a major irrigation system. We prefer to have our water to try to save our large alfalfa fields. Because of that, we are at odds with other communities.

We are also having discussions with our neighbors about the water itself even within our own community because as a farmer, a lot of times we take our grandkids out there to teach them how to irrigate. Guess what, they love to play in the water and they get wet.

The question is, is the water really safe now that we have been hit with this disaster? The mothers and grandmothers especially ask that question. What happens?

I think these are the social issues for those who have been impacted and had this inflicted upon us. It is going to take a long time to get over this.

Thank you.

The CHAIRMAN. Dr. Weindorf, in your written testimony, you state that the water "will likely appear quite clear and usable but the likelihood of small amounts of metals contained in the slowly migrating sludge will have the potential to accumulate in farm fields over time." Is that an accurate assessment of what you said?

Mr. WEINDORF. Yes, sir.

The CHAIRMAN. You urge, of course, careful observation, recommend clean up of the sludge in areas where it is apparent and accessible. In your opinion, is the EPA not focusing enough on the health risks and potential impacts to the communities of the sludge moving downstream and into the irrigation ditches?

Mr. WEINDORF. I would say I was really taken aback when I was there in New Mexico making assessments with the NRCS and New Mexico State at the overall lack of emphasis being put on things.

I know there are people in the area working on things but using older, traditional methods. They are collecting soil samples, sending those off to a lab and waiting for weeks for those results to come back. It is a spot check here or there.

We come on site with our technology and are able to do 140 sites in different places in three days. In fact, when the rancher or farmer is out there, they want to see the results while I am scanning right there. They can see it on the screen themselves which I think speaks to a lot of what the President mentioned here, the distrust of the data that comes back. Wouldn't it be nice for them to see that data right there on the screen?

I think there is a serious concern about the accumulation of these metals over time. One of the things I was shocked about when I went to the Colorado Res, you see this red sludge all along the edge of the river that is still there today. I worry about that eroding away and slowly working its way into the river.

When we had the Exxon Valdez spill, we had people out there in chemical suits washing the rocks. When we had the Deep Water Horizon spill, I was there on-site. People used chemical suits. They were literally scooping up the sludge.

Why is that not happening with the sludge in the river? All you have to do is look at these photos I brought with me today to see the material is clearly there. It is red. It is as obvious as can be.

I really take issue with the fact that there was testimony given earlier today that these levels have returned to pre-spill levels. I dispute that.

I think there is a concern moving forward. I think it is a legitimate concern and warrants careful monitoring.

The CHAIRMAN. Mr. Holtz-Eakin, according to Navajo officials the unemployment rate for the Navajo Nation tribal members is at 42 percent. Your testimony noted that agriculture is a primary economic driver for the reservation. As a result, farming and ranching communities have taken a direct hit because of the EPA spill devastating the tribal economy for a long time.

In your opinion, has the EPA's actions adequately mitigated the economic and health threats to the farming and ranching community to ensure long term viability of the tribe's economy?

Mr. HOLTZ-EAKIN. I do not think so to this date. If you listen to the testimony you just heard, they are leaving the sludge exposed. That is the environmental danger that leads to a health danger that undermines the economic confidence of anyone doing business with the Navajo Nation, so no.

The CHAIRMAN. I thank each and every one of you.

I want to go to Senator Udall. I think you have a written statement from someone who is not on the panel but you want to include that? I would like to turn it over to you

Senator UDALL. Thank you very much, Chairman Barrasso.

Let me thank you again because you have been very thorough about this hearing and very patient in terms of getting in all the testimony. I really appreciate it. I appreciate the entire panel being here.

We have one additional person who I mentioned earlier. He is a chapter president, Chili Yazzi. I talked to the Chairman and he wants to proceed under the rules and I understand. Chili Yazzi has done a statement, President Begaye, as you know. I am going to read his statement into the record.

This is from the chapter president. This chapter, as President Begaye knows, was very impacted.

"I greet you as relatives, as five-fingered human beings and as brothers and sisters of the same earth mother and the same father creator. Through our ways of reverence, we have our special names for the great creator, including God the Almighty.

We know him as Dzan. Our creator stories say he formed mounds of clay and breathed life into them. Thus, we have an intrinsic and undeniable relationship with the earth. We are of the earth and we return to the earth. The earth belongs to all of us and we belong to the earth just as a child and a mother belong to each other.

The teachings of our peoples concur in that God is everywhere. God the Creator inhabits the vast expanse of his creation. His essence permeates through the earth. Thus, the earth has spirit, it has life, it breathes and feels pain as we do.

It is no misnomer that we refer to her as our earth mother. She has unfailingly provided for all our needs but we are failing her as the stewards we are supposed to be. As parents, we have an unconditional love for our children and as grandparents, we have the greatest hopes for the future of our grandchildren. That is our common bond. We may have traveled different paths of history but we have a common future in humankind and we share a common destiny.

Our indigenous choice is that we want our earth to survive as her life is our life. It is clear that exponentially increasing exploitation of the earth is ebbing her life and thus, accelerating the closure of our collective life.

As the original landlords of these lands, we stand in defense of our earth. We choose to defend her life and the light of our life. We implore of you, with a focus on the future of our coming generations, let us reason together, let us stand together for the life of our earth mother and the lives of our children.''

That was Chapter President Yazzie. As President Begaye knows, the chapter is the local form of government. His chapter as very impacted by this. His name is Duane Chili Yazzi. I would ask his full statement be put in the record.

I appreciate your courtesy, Mr. Chairman.

The CHAIRMAN. Thank you, Senator Udall.

I would just ask the members of the panel, are there any final statements, things you might say if the Administrator had actually stayed to hear your testimony?

Mr. BEGAYE. Thank you, Mr. Chairman.

I just want to say that our Navajo Nation has suffered greatly and continue to suffer. We want the services returned that have been taken away, the water tanks and the hay feed because our farmers have truly lost a lot.

This will impact them the whole winter. They spent monies they do not have. These are monies to pay bills and buy clothes for their children and school supplies. All of that is now gone. They have been devastated and they need to be compensated very quickly.

I am asking this Committee and the EPA to set up an emergency fund to be used to compensate our farmers and our ranchers on a very timely basis. We are asking for that and they have asked me to say that over and over and over.

I am speaking for my people and for these ranchers who have been hurt. They need these dollars now.

Thank you.

The CHAIRMAN. Thank you.

Mr. Olguin?

Mr. OLGUIN. Thank you.

In closing, I would like to say is we as Ute people, whether the Southern Ute people or the Ute Mountain Ute people or even the

Northern Ute people, we roamed those mountains. That was our homeland. We were removed from those mountains because of the gold, the minerals and the need for the silver.

Along that line, the mining industry has impacted us for hundreds of years. Today, it still continues to impact us. I think it is important that we understand there is a need for a government-to-government relationship, whether it is one tribe or all tribes because each tribe is being treated differently.

We are treated differently than the Navajo, than Ute Mountain. Ute Mountain still has concerns with EPA's lack of response. They wanted me to share that so I am taking that opportunity. They are asking for EPA to respond to their needs which is the uranium mine at Mill Creek.

I think it is very important that the relationship be fostered and be maintained. Of course, funding is of utmost importance, that the EPA provide that funding for cleanup of these types of spills and accidents.

Thank you.

The CHAIRMAN. Thank you.

Mr. Holtz-Eakin?

Mr. HOLTZ-EAKIN. No.

The CHAIRMAN. Mr. Weindorf?

Mr. WEINDORF. You have heard repeatedly today that there is deep-seated mistrust of the U.S. Environmental Protection Agency. I would encourage the panel to engage with the U.S. Department of Agriculture, specifically the Natural Resources Conservation Service.

This is an agency that is trusted and has a long history of working with farmers in the area. I think you will find every time we came on-site and said we were working with NRCS, the residents gave us a pat on the back, thank you so much for being here, we really appreciate the help you are providing to us.

These were the conservation partners with the legacy of helping to protect our land and resources.

Also, I would encourage the panel to engage with academicians at the university level with specialized expertise in the latest research going on in these areas and include people like Dr. Lombard who personally lives in the area impacted and has expertise to lend in that regard.

Thank you so much.

The CHAIRMAN. Thank you.

Mr. Harrison, you get the last word.

Mr. HARRISON. Thank you very much.

I just wanted to say many, many times farmers and ranchers live in rural areas of America. We are forgotten many times. We hear talk about the Administrator, how they can do all these things but many times at the fear level. You do not see results and that is what is concerning.

Finally, we look to the Congress, to Senators and Representatives to help us, the little people. We are not asking for a bunch. We are just saying keep an eye out for us.

Thank you very much.

The CHAIRMAN. I thank each and every one of you. Thank you all for being here today. Thank you for your time. Thank you for your testimony.

There may be some written questions submitted. The record will remain open for the next two weeks.

I appreciate all of you being here and sharing your stories with us today and your expertise.

The hearing is adjourned.

[Whereupon, at 4:39 p.m., the Committee was adjourned.]

APPENDIX

PREPARED STATEMENT OF LORENZO BATES, NAVAJO NATION COUNCIL DELEGATE FOR THE COMMUNITIES OF NENAHNEZAD, NEWCOMB, SAN JUAN, TIIS TSOH SIKAAD, TSE'DAA'KAAN, AND UPPER FRUITLAND

Yáá'át'ééh Chairman Barrasso, Vice-Chairman Tester, and Members of the Committee, my name is LoRenzo Bates. I am the Council Delegate for the communities of Nenahnezad, Newcomb, San Juan, Tiis Tsoh Sikaad, Tse'Daa'Kaan, and Upper Fruitland. Each of these communities have been impacted by the spill, but Nenahnezad, San Juan, Upper Fruitland, and Tse'Daa'Kaan all lie directly along the path of the San Juan River. The other communities that I serve all draw water from directly or indirectly from the river for human and agricultural use. Thank you for the opportunity to submit testimony to the committee on a matter of great significance to the Navajo Nation on behalf of the communities and the farmers I represent.

On August 5, 2015, Environmental Restoration, LLC (herein "Environmental Restoration"), a contractor for the U.S. Environmental Protection Agency (herein "USEPA") was attempting to contain a leak from the Gold King Mine near Silverton, Colorado. The contractor using heavy machinery ruptured the mine's containment barrier releasing millions of gallons of contaminated mine waste into a tributary of the Animas River, Cement Creek. This toxic wastewater containing heavy metals such as arsenic, lead, and cadmium flowed from Cement Creek into the Animas River, and into the San Juan River (herein "SJR").

The SJR in northern New Mexico flows for more than 200 miles through Navajo Country. The SJR provides almost all of the water for the Navajo communities that live along it. The SJR was subject to a federally mandates water settlement in 2008 that finalized the Navajo Nation and the State of New Mexico's water claims as well authorized the construction of a water development project that will carry water from the San Juan River to Gallup, NM and then to Window Rock, AZ, serving all the Navajo communities in between.

The full impact of this spill into the rivers of the Navajo Nation will not be known for years. However, in the near term the Navajo Communities along the river have experienced significant cultural and economic damages as a result of the spill. Water is sacred to the Navajo People; it is the basis of all life. Spiritually and culturally Navajo beliefs are deeply connected to the land, air, and water that lie between the four sacred mountains that form the aboriginal boundary of our land. These connections are reinforced spiritually in the ceremonies that comprise Navajo beliefs. Our ceremonies use traditional seeds and crops that are grown and gathered on Navajo land. The spill has contaminated or destroyed many of the essential elements of our religious practice, and desecrated a river we have treated with reverence since time immemorial.

Water is essential to our survival as a species, and is the foundation of our agricultural economy. The Navajo Nation is located in the high desert Four Corners region of the southwest and is approximately the size of West Virginia. As an arid environment, the loss of any water access for the communities is both life threatening and economically devastating. The Navajo Nation is still mainly an agrarian society that relies predominantly on the raising of livestock, mainly sheep, and the growth of crops such as corn. The SJR and the irrigation ditches serve the farming and ranching communities along the river provide nearly all of the water essential for watering livestock and irrigating crops. The spill that occurred on August 5 unfortunately happened at the peak of our growing season. As a result of the inability to irrigate crops many of the farmers along the San Juan River have been devastated by the loss of an entire season of crops. Ranchers were forced to watch their sheep and cattle suffer from the inability to water, and may have lost animals directly, and be both unable to survive off, or sell for profit, the stunted animals that remain.

These are small family farms and ranches that grow enough to provide for their own needs and a small amount left over to allow for sale into the surrounding communities. As anyone who has spent time around farmers and ranchers can tell you, agriculture is not for the faint of heart. Seasonal variations of sun, rain, and snow, acts of God, and random occurrences all come together to influence the lottery of a good or bad season. The emotional and economic swings that frame a life in agriculture mean that our farmers and ranchers are used to dealing with these challenges. However, this was a manmade act by an agent of the Federal Government.

The secondary impacts of these economic losses are only just beginning. The Navajo Nation as a whole has an unemployment rate that very often hovers at 50 percent. We have a per capita income around $7,000. Among the communities with a strong agricultural or fossil fuel backbone, the impact of these devastatingly low levels of employment and income are mitigated. However, the economic ripples created by this spill will continue to cause a loss of jobs and income for years to come. Unfortunately, with this rise in unemployment and the emotional desperation that it causes we are also expecting to see a rise in social problems such as domestic and substance abuse.

Similarly, the long-term impact of the spill resulting from contamination of the river, sediment, and surrounding land is potentially catastrophic. We know that the toxic sludge plume has passed through the SJR and into Lake Powell. We also know that the plume itself moved at a much slower rate than the river that carried it. Therefore, the water of the SJR, which was highly contaminated as the plume moved along its path, is more than likely clear at this point. Any damages from the water alone were caused by the inability to use the water during the closure of the river, diversions, and irrigation ditches.

Contaminates that moved slowly through the water had a substantial ability to contaminate the sediment of the river for generations to come. These contaminates have not passed, they are persisting in the ecosystem contaminating its base and lying in wait for an event to bring them back into the stream flow. The introduction of contaminates such as lead, arsenic, and cadmium, among other contaminates, into the ecosystem and food chain of the river will have untold effects on the river, the communities that subsist on the river, and the economies of those communities for years. As a result, the Federal Government will have to commit to both long-term clean up and monitoring of the river and its ecosystem.

Of greater concern than the contamination of the river itself are the long-term health effects of these toxic chemicals on people and animals. The toxins released during the spill will persist in the ecosystem. Lead, arsenic, and cadmium are known to cause birth and developmental damage in humans and livestock. EPA data from tests of the water found exposure levels hundreds and thousands of times beyond federal safe levels for humans. Now that these toxins are in the food chain they could contaminate wildlife and livestock and eventually the people that rely on them for food.

While the USEPA certainly made mistakes in communication, protocol, and compensation during the early response to this disaster, further highlighting these mistakes here does little to advance the needs of the communities or the clean-up efforts. The community members have reported a dramatic turnaround in how the USEPA has dealt with victims of the spill.

The Navajo People have suffered significantly as a result of these actions and will continue to suffer from the environmental, health, and economic effects of the spill for years to come. The Federal Government must find a way to quickly and efficiently compensate those who have been affected by the spill and provide for the long-term health and clean up of the SJR and its surrounding ecosystem. The Navajo Nation has long worked closely with the USEPA to develop and enforce rules and regulations that protect our water, air, and land while providing us with the greatest opportunities for self-determination. While the effect of this spill and its response has shaken the Navajo Nation's faith in the USEPA, the USEPA has responded by working closely with the Navajo Nation Council and the affected communities. I thank them for their efforts and look forward to a full restoration of our working relationship as they begin to address the clean up and monitoring of the river, and the health of those at risk for contamination. Frequent communication and prompt compensation for those effected by the spill has done much to alleviate the concerns of the community.

We look forward to working closely with the USEPA and the Federal Government to address the needs of the Navajo communities and the environment today, and in the long term. The problems that have defined the initial response, clean up and compensation do not need to taint the future response and cooperation between the Navajo Nation, the USEPA, and the Federal Government. The Navajo Nation looks forward to working closely with this committee and the Congress to ensure future needs and communications are handled in a timely and proper manner.

PREPARED STATEMENT OF NANCY FREEMAN, EXECUTIVE DIRECTOR, GROUND WATER AWARENESS LEAGUE

Dear Committee Members,

Thank you for your recent hearing on harmful impacts to indian Country. I am submitting additional comments regarding issues that were brought up in the hearing regarding oversight by Government Agencies.

Somehow the EPA and DOI are not taking responsibility for the travesties created on the Native American lands and their water supply in the rush to mine uranium that was sold only to the U.S. government. There have been extensive harmful impacts on water and land due to in the Navajo nation and other Native American lands due to mining.

I know for a fact that the regulations and precautions on the Native American lands was not the same as in off-reservation lands. I know this because I live near Twin Buttes mine in Sahuarita, Arizona where yellow cake uranium was mined and produced for 20 years. I know miners who worked there. They had safety equipment and precautions that were not used on the Native American mines. EPA has had continual oversight there though its closing.

I did write a report to Congress several years ago highlighting the problem and hardly anything has changes. The Newmont Mining Company has finally agreed to clean-up the Spokane Reservation site, but not much as been accomplished during the first five-year plan:

http://mining-law-reform.info/Urgency.htm

In addition, I am submitting my recent comments for your edification to DOI regarding their recent hearings on the royalties for coal mining on BLM/Native American Reservation lands.

https://www.youtube.com/watch?v=0wy1LeBMHUk&feature=youtu.be

Comments on Coal Royalties

First issue: Increasing coal royalty rate to 18.75 percent to match that of other federally-owned fossil fuels.

Of course, this issue is a logical policy that should be implemented. My concern is will the Native Americans be treated as other private landowners? Since I live in Arizona, I have researched and found a lot of evidence using the situation with the Dine (Navajos) that the Native Americans are not treated equally or fairly.

The Navajo Nation land is a National Disaster Area. When will the betrayal of the Navajo Nation by the U.S. Government through the funnel of the Department of Interior end? Currently, there are three coal power plants polluting the air, land and water on the Navajo Nation. One is on the northeast border. The other two send power as far as Los Angeles, while 40 percent of the Navajos do not have electricity in their homes.

The DOI has processed permits for coal mines and power plants without a full disclosure of the health risks and without requiring that the plants to use OSHA standards. Did the DOI agents explain to the workers the pollutants they would be inhaling, did they explain to the community the pollutants that would be in the air on their crops, their water supplies and in their lungs? Did they explain to the community members why they would not be hooked up to power, when it was possible to send power to Los Angeles?

In addition coal power uses water. The U.S. Government can permit unlimited water use for the coal plants, even without any disclosure to the Navajo Nation, yet the U.S. has not formulated a reasonable, just water settlement for the Navajo Nation. In 2003, the Government rejected the carefully planned Water Settlement that the Navajo and Hopi Governments had drawn up. The Arizona Senators then filed a settlement that divided the interests of the Navajo and Hopi, just as the U.S. Government has done with the reservation boundaries. At this time, the Navajo do not have rights to the Little Colorado River that runs across their Nation, yet the DOI allowed Peabody Energy to use from the Navajo Aquifer.

How can the Navajo and 79 other tribes trust DOI to them adequately? The mismanagement of payments for trust leases was well illustrated in the Cobell v. Babbitt, Kempthorne, Norton, Salazar lawsuit over trust payments for leases that took 21 years for the Department of Interior to finalize. In fact, the proceedings in Cobell v. et al exposed a tragic pattern of mismanagement, neglect, malfeasance and attitude of not caring for over a century. The lies and cover ups by the DOI officials put forth in a Federal trial concerning a class of 500,000 plaintiffs who had been cheated were shocking. The Government could not even produce the trust documents for the five named plaintiffs in the case. The Government had agreed to produce these documents by March of 1997. But with their records in complete disarray, they failed to produce documents for any of the named plaintiffs after four years of court. In the face of "clear and convincing evidence," Judge Lamberth held DOI Secretary Babbitt, Treasury Secretary Robert Rubin, and Assistant DOI Secretary Gover in civil contempt.

The Honorable Judge Lamberth described the situation:

> The entire record in this case tells the dreary story of Interior's degenerate tenure as Trustee—Delegate for the Indian trust—a story shot through with bureaucratic blunders, flubs, goofs and foul-ups, and peppered with scandals, deception, dirty tricks and outright villainy—the end of which is nowhere in sight. Despite the breadth and clarity of this record, Interior continues to litigate and re-litigate, in excruciating fashion, every minor, technical detail.

> The response of the Government (with its 100 attorneys working against the Native Americans) was to request the removal of Judge Lamberth from the case. In 2003, ten years after the filing of the case, which turned out to be good because other judges were brought into the case and the ruled exactly as Lamberth had.

> In addition to the withholding of trust payments, several situations of outright fraud by the Government "overseers" were brought out in the proceedings. In particular, for a pipeline "right-of-way" across the San Juan Basin, Navajo allotted land was valued at $25–30 per "rod" (at 16.6-foot unit), whereas neighboring tribal land was valued at $140–$575 per rod, and land belonging to private landowners at $432–$455 per rod. Navajo allottees were cheated, in violation of the Government's fiduciary obligations, plus federal law mandating "just compensation" for such land use.

> Another example cited in the proceedings was on Shoshone land in Idaho, which includes prime agricultural property, had been valued at $65 to $75 per acre. Meanwhile, non-Native Americans living adjacent to this property are receiving over $200 per acre for the same use. The problem is that Government officials appraise Native American land without looking at "non-Indian comparables." By only looking at records of leases on other Native American leases, the undervaluation of leases for Native American lands, as compared with non-Native American lands, is self-perpetuating. Judge Lamberth lamented:

> But regardless of the motivations of the originators of the trust, one would expect, or at least hope, that the modern Interior department and its modern administrators would manage it in a way that reflects our modern understandings of how the Government should treat people. Alas, our "modem" Interior department has time and again demonstrated that it is a dinosaur—the morally and culturally oblivious hand-me-down of a disgracefully racist and imperialist Government that should have been buried a century ago, the last pathetic outpost of the indifference and Anglo-centrism we thought we had left behind.

We know for a fact that the coal leases manipulated by DOI on Navajo lands. In 1963 when BLM and DOI negotiated coal contracts on the Navajo Nation land they gave the Navajos an unheard of low rate for coal. I would also like to see the comparisons of coal royalties paid to other tribes and non-tribal lands at that time.

Since DOI/BLM's underpayment continued, when Peter MacDonald became the tribe's chairman in 1971, he went on a campaign to get Peabody to pay the tribe a fair amount for royalties for its coal mining operations. MacDonald pointed out that the tribe was only receiving 20 cents a ton royalty from the company, about the cost of a can of Coke (in 1971). MacDonald and tribal attorneys would after several years get a new agreement from Peabody that would sharply increase the tribe's share to 12.5 percent of the value of the coal at the mine site.

To make matters worse Peabody used a slurry line, not the usual railway to convey coal to Nevada. The Navajos lost 30,000 acre feet of water from their aquifer with no consent or compensation. To make matters worse, Interior Secretary Udall covered for Peabody by stating the compensation for the water was in the royalty (20 cents per ton)!

Increase of royalty rate to match other fossil fuel rates is a clear statement that you have been undercharging the coal prices on Federal Land, cheating U.S. Taxpayers, but more egregiously cheating Native Americans.

One would think that after the long drawn-out Cobell Trust Settlements (1993–2014) in which the courts showed that the malfeasance and downright criminal injustices to the Native Americans that the DOI would mend their ways. However, I see no evidence that it is happening. The legacy of mining on the Navajo Nation land is a truly egregious story of criminal injustices by the U.S. Government through Department of Interior but of course it is not the only agency, but it appears to be the leader, setting an example for others.

It appears that the Navajos receive no power from two of the dirtiest coal-fired power plants in the country. The Navajo Generating Station (NGS) in Page, Arizona and the Four Corners Power Plant near Shiprock, New Mexico—are among the country's top emitters of carbon dioxide, releasing 17.8 million short tons and 12.9 million short tons in 2013, respectively. Even though they have to bear this load of pollution, it is estimated that 40 percent of the Navajos are without any power to their homes.

I cannot find the exact users of the APS Four Corners Plant, but it appears that the Navajos do not receive any power from its presence.

The owners of the Four Corners APS power plant:

Units 1, 2, and 3
Arizona Public Service Company (APS) 100 percent
Units 4 and 5
APS 63 percent
Public Service Company of New Mexico 13 percent
Salt River Project 10 percent
Tucson Electric Power 7 percent
El Paso Electric 7 percent

The Navajos definitely receive no power, only pollution from the Navajo Generating Station.

Users of NGS power:

U.S. Bureau of Reclamation (Central Arizona Project water) 24.3 percent
Salt River Project (residential) 21.7 percent
Los Angeles Dept. of Water and Power 21.2 percent
Arizona Public Service Co. (residential) 14.0 percent
NV [Nevada] Energy 11.3 percent
Tucson Electric Power 7.5 percent

When EPA announced more stringent equipment to control toxic pollutants the CAP officials of Arizona gave presentations showing that the equipment would double the price of water to Arizona citizens-so the pollution should be continued as is even though the citizens would not want to live in the toxic plume of a coal power plant.

The DOI needs to assure that the coal companies have a consultation with Native Americans before any removal of any of the Native American ancestral bones and artifacts, so that the Native Americans can retain their ancestral property. In 1967 Peabody Energy (NGS coal plant) needed to clear land it was leasing on the Navajo reservation to mine the coal, but ancient Indian dwellings and graves were in the way. So, as required by law, it did hire archeologists who dug up roughly 1.3 million Navajo, Hopi and ancient Anasazi artifacts—including the remains of 200 Native Americans—which have been warehoused at two universities ever since. The Navajos were not involved in the actions or decisions. They are still attempting to get the bodies of their ancestors returned, so that they can be give them a proper burial.

Another recent betrayal of the Navajos was that when Obama released the carbon reduction plan he left out power plants on the Native American lands. This omission leaves the Native Americans to fend for themselves, without having in regulatory power at all over the power plants, that's not part of their "sovereignty." The Navajo Nation already has set standards for sulfur dioxide, particulate matter and nitrogen oxide emissions from power plants on the reservation. However, what will they mean to the companies who have been with no oversight for years.

However, EPA does keep records of the Toxics that are released to the environment: Not surprisingly, the numbers are high. The releases are given in pounds. There are no numbers for uranium and its daughters, such as radon. As is too well known, uranium is prevalent on Navajo land with over 500 abandoned, un-reclaimed mines there.

Data Source: EPA TRI Database:
*http://iaspub.epa.gov/triexplorer/re-
lease\fac?sort=\VIEW\&trilib=TRIQ1&sort\fmt=1&state=TS&county=Navajo
percent20Nation, percent20Arizona, percent20New percent20Mexico percent20and
percent20Utah&chemical=All+chemicals&industry=ALL&year=
2013&plview=TIFA&tab\rpt=1&fld=RELLBY&fld=TSFDSP*

Second Issue: Closing loopholes that let coal companies avoid paying some royalties by selling coal through their subsidiaries.

This action needs to be taken.

Third Issue: Updating agency policies to make sure that potential profits from coal exports are considered in setting the market value.

This action needs to be taken with the assurance that the Native American tribes will be compensated at the same rate as other coal leases.

Fourth Issue: Updating policies related to bonding to prevent taxpayers from being stuck with hundreds of millions of dollars in mining cleanup fees.

This is of utmost importance. In a hearing yesterday of the Senate Committee on Indian Affairs this issue was brought up. Many of the boom and bust mining companies have disappeared. However, there is also a challenge in getting existing companies to clean up their mines—hiding under the excuse of Dawn mining, which declared bankruptcy, was a subsidiary. I just received an update from a environmental friend on the Spokane Reservation that has been fighting for years for a clean up of historic uranium mines there. Twa-le wrote,

> That link is to the case summary, I just re-read it and saw that DOI is actually covering the cleanup costs for the role they played. The BIA has almost been nonexistent in this entire process. They are just assuming ⅓ of the responsibility and during the long drawn out legal process, Newmont was also trying to hold the Tribe and individual landowners responsible as well. So, it was a long drawn out case, they had the resources to fight and the Spokane Tribe spent many years and lots of resources alongside EPA to get the clean up moving. The latest update: *http://www.wise-uranium.org/udmif.html*
> Source: Twa-le Abrahamson, Spokane Tribe,Spokane, Washington, Natural Resources Dept. Manager, Air Quality Dept.

I honestly don't think bonding is enough for a bankrupt company. There has to be real money banked up front. Also, I recommend that a company that is not in environmental compliance, reclamation compliance of financial liquidity should not be permitted. The Spokane Reservation mine operated by subsidiary Dawn is a good example. Newmont should not be given any permit for mining until it has done due diligence in its reclamation of the Spokane Reservation. They are five years into their reclamation plan and nothing is happening on the ground.

Thank you for your attention to these serious matters of the treatment of the Native Americans. I am filing some FOIA's to get some data on the past royalty payments and comparables with other public lands—and private lands. Note the example above of the Shoshone Tribe where DOI was not using public comparables, but the lower rates historically given to Native Americans.

————

PREPARED STATEMENT OF HON. DUANE "CHILI" YAZZIE, CHAPTER PRESIDENT, NAVAJO NATION

I greet you as relatives, as five fingered human beings, as brothers and sisters of the same Earth Mother and the same Father Creator. Through our ways of reverence we have our special names for the Great Creator including God the Almighty; we know Him as Diyin. Our creation stories say He formed mounds of clay and breathed life into them. Thus we have an intrinsic and undeniably relationship with the Earth, we are of the Earth and we return to the Earth. The Earth belongs to all of us and we belong to the Earth, just as a child and mother belong to each other.

The teachings of our peoples concur in that God is everywhere, God the Creator inhabits the vast expanse of His creation. His essence permeates through the Earth, thus the Earth has spirit, it has life, it breathes and feels pain as we do. It is no misnomer that we refer to her as our Earth Mother. She has unfailingly provided for all our needs but we are failing her as the stewards we supposed to be.

As parents we have an unconditional love for our children and as grandparents we have the greatest hopes for the future of our grandchildren; that is our common bond. We may have traveled different paths of history but we have a common future, as humankind we share a common destiny.

As Indigenous Peoples we retain and maintain the Original Intent, by choice we choose to live in the world our Creator made, a world where the physical and spiritual realms remain intact as one reality. The Creator intended for there to be a balance in all of nature, but today the equilibrium of the world is precariously out of balance. The bursting of toxic waste into our life giving rivers is a message we cannot ignore, the unmitigated exploitation of the world must end; the damage to the Earth caused by this exploitation must be repaired.

The changing conditions of our Earth cannot be denied; the pollution, drought, wild fires, melting glaciers, rising oceans and the increasing scarcity of water the world over. It is urgently imperative that we protect our waters. These adverse changes impact us all, it is our responsibility to come together with parity to talk about these great concerns. What should our priorities be? Jobs and economics or our need to protect the Earth or can a balance be achieved.

Our Indigenous choice is that we want our Earth to survive, as her life is our life. It is clear to us that the exponentially increasing exploitation of the Earth is ebbing her life and thus, accelerating the closure of our collective life. As the original Landlords of these lands we stand in defense of our Earth; we choose to defend her life and the life of all life. We implore of you with a focus on the future of our coming generations, let us reason together. Let us stand together for the life of our Earth Mother and the lives of all her children.

RESPONSE TO WRITTEN QUESTIONS SUBMITTED BY HON. JAMES LANKFORD TO HON. GINA MCCARTHY

1. Please provide the copy of the rule entitled "National Ambient Air Quality Standards for Ozone", originally published in the Federal Register as a proposed rule on December 17, 2014, as it appeared when it was transmitted to the Office of Management and Budget for final review on or about August 28, 2015.

RESPONSE: The initial submittal of the rule to the Office of Management and Budget is publicly available at: http://www.regulations.gov/index.jsp#!documentDetail;D=EPA-HQ-OAR-2008-0699-4482.

2. Please provide a redline copy including all changes made by the Office of Management and Budget during review of the proposed final rule entitled "National Ambient Air Quality Standards for Ozone" upon completion of their review of the final rule.

RESPONSE: A redline and clean version of the rule is publicly available at: http://www.regulations.gov/#!documentDetail;D=EPA-HQ-OAR-2008-0699-4360.

3. The SBA's Office of Advocacy, which ensures compliance with the Regulatory Flexibility Act (RFA) and SBREFA, wrote the following to EPA in October 2014: "Section 605(b) of the RFA allows an agency to certify that a rule will not have a significant economic impact on a substantial number of small entities in lieu of preparing an IRFA. When certifying, the agency must provide a factual basis for the certification. In the current case, the agencies have certified that revising the definition of "waters of the United States" will not have a significant economic impact on a substantial number of small businesses." Among the arguments that the SBA Office of Advocacy used included (1) that the agency used an incorrect baseline for determining their RFA obligations, (2) that the rule imposes costs directly on small businesses, and (3) that the rule will have a significant economic impact on small businesses.

   a. Can you explain how EPA decided to certify that WOTUS would not have a significant economic impact on a substantial number of small entities?

RESPONSE: Under the RFA, the impact of concern is any significant *adverse* economic impact on small entities, because the primary purpose of the initial regulatory flexibility analysis is to identify and address regulatory alternatives "which minimize any significant economic impact of the proposed rule on small entities." 5 U.S.C. 603. The scope of jurisdiction in the final Clean Water Rule is narrower than that under the existing regulations. See 40 CFR 122.2 (defining "waters of the United States"). Because fewer waters would be subject to the CWA under the Clean Water Rule than are subject to regulation under the prior regulations, the EPA determined that this action would not affect small entities to a greater degree than the prior regulations.

The Clean Water Rule is not designed to "subject" any entities of any size to any specific regulatory burden. Rather, it is designed to clarify the statutory scope of "the waters of the United States, including the territorial seas," section 502(7), consistent with Supreme Court precedent. This question of CWA jurisdiction is informed by the tools of statutory construction and the geographical and hydrological factors identified in *Rapanos v. United States*, 547 U.S. 715 (2006), which are not factors readily informed by the RFA.

Nevertheless, the scope of the term "waters of the United States" is a question that has continued to generate substantial interest, particularly within the small business community, because permits must be obtained for many discharges of pollutants into those waters. In light of this interest, the EPA and the Army determined to seek wide input from representatives of small entities while formulating the proposed and final definition of this term that reflects the intent of Congress consistent with the mandate of the Supreme Court's decisions. Such outreach, although voluntary, is also consistent with the President's January 18, 2011 Memorandum on Regulatory Flexibility, Small Business, and Job Creation, which emphasizes the important role small businesses play in the American economy.

This process enabled the agencies to hear directly from these representatives, throughout the rule development, about how they should approach this complex question of statutory interpretation. The agencies prepared a report summarizing their small entity outreach, the results of this outreach, and how these results informed the development of this rule. This report, Report of the Discretionary Small Entity Outreach for the Revised Definition of Waters of the United States (Docket Id. No. EPA–HQ–OW–2011–0880–1927), is available in the docket.

4. On April 27, 2015, U.S. Army Major General John W. Peabody drafted a memorandum outlining the "serious concerns" the Corps of Engineers had with aspects of the draft final rule of "Waters of the United States (WOTUS)." The Major General indicated that the final draft rule,

...Continues to depart significantly from the version provided for public comment, and that the Corps' recommendations related to our most serious concerns have gone unaddressed. Specifically, the current draft final rule contradicts long-standing and well-established legal principles undergirding Clean Water Act (CWA) Section 404 regulations and regulatory practices, especially the decisive Rapanos Supreme Court decision. The rule's contradictions with legal principles generate multiple legal and technical consequences that, in the view of the Corps, would be fatal to the rule in its current form.

As requested during the hearing, please provide the written legal analysis contained in e-mails, memoranda, and letters that the EPA drafted in response to the Army's concerns expressed above.

RESPONSE: The document to which your question refers is a deliberative memo internal to the Department of the Army. The EPA did not receive a copy of the memo until it was provided to Congress, which was after the Clean Water Rule was promulgated. The EPA did not prepare any written legal analysis of the memo.

5. After April 27, 2015, what portions of the draft WOTUS rule were changed because the Army Corps expressed concerns?

RESPONSE: Issues raised by the Army Corps of Engineers were considered during the development of the rule, and the final rule represents the policy decisions of both the Administrator of the EPA and the Assistant Secretary of the Army for Civil Works.

A number of revisions were made between the proposed rule and the final rule based on the Corps' concerns. As Assistant Secretary of the Army Jo-Ellen Darcy testified before the U.S. Senate Committee on Environment and Public Works on September 30, 2015, the Army Corps of Engineers is "unequivocally committed to implementing the new rule as effectively and efficiently as possible."

6. Did the public have the opportunity to evaluate the WOTUS 4000-feet cut-off line (or "bright line rule") or to comment on it during the public comment period? If so, please explain.

RESPONSE: In the proposal, the agencies sought comment on a number of ways to address and clarify jurisdiction including establishing a floodplain interval and providing clarity on reasonable proximity as an important aspect of adjacency.

7. What is the scientific and legal basis for establishing the 4000-feet from the ordinary high water mark or high tide line as the Clean Water Act (CWA) jurisdictional cut-off line?

RESPONSE: The agencies viewed a strong science foundation as a condition precedent to any revision to the definition of the term "waters of the United States." The EPA report entitled "Connectivity of Streams and Wetlands to Downstream Waters: A Review and Synthesis of the Scientific Evidence" (Science Report) represents the state-of-the-science on the connectivity and isolation of waters in the United States. The Science Report was developed using only peer-reviewed science, and the report itself was subject to multiple peer reviews, including review by the independent EPA Science Advisory Board.

The Supreme Court's decisions in *Riverside Bayview, SWANCC,* and *Rapanos* provided critical context and guidance in determining the appropriate scope of "waters of the United States" covered by the CWA. In the rule, the agencies interpreted the scope of "waters of the United States" for the CWA in light of the goals, objectives, and policies of the statute, the Supreme Court case law, the relevant and available science, and the agencies' technical expertise and experience.

As the agencies stated in the preamble, what constitutes a significant nexus is not a purely scientific determination. The opinions of the Supreme Court have noted that as the agencies charged with interpreting the statute, the EPA and the Corps must develop the outer bounds of the scope of the CWA, while science does not provide bright line boundaries with respect to where "water ends" for purposes of the CWA. In addition, the agencies responded to the need to make the process of identifying waters protected under the CWA easier to understand, more predictable, and consistent with the law and peer-reviewed science.

8. Did the public have the opportunity to evaluate or publically comment upon EPA's definitional change of the term "adjacent" in WOTUS? If so, when was this opportunity?

RESPONSE: In the proposal, the agencies sought comment on a number of ways to address and clarify jurisdiction over "adjacent waters," including establishing a floodplain interval and providing clarity on reasonable proximity as an important aspect of adjacency. In light of the comments, the science, the agencies' experience, and the Supreme Court's consistent recognition of the agencies' discretion to interpret the bounds of CWA jurisdiction, the agencies made some revisions in the final rule designed to more clearly establish boundaries on the scope of "adjacent waters."

The proposal included wetlands, ponds, lakes, and impoundments that contribute flow, directly or indirectly, to the downstream traditional navigable waters, interstate waters, or the territorial seas in the definition of "tributary." Some commenters expressed concern that since such waters generally do not have both an ordinary high water mark and a bed and banks, the definition of tributary was contradictory and confusing.

9. What is the scientific and legal basis for EPA's definitional revision of the term "adjacent" in WOTUS?

RESPONSE: The agencies viewed a strong science foundation as a condition precedent to any revision to the definition of the term "waters of the United States." The EPA report entitled "Connectivity of Streams and Wetlands to Downstream Waters: A Review and Synthesis of the Scientific Evidence" (Science Report) represents the state-of-the-science on the connectivity and isolation of waters in the United States. The Science Report was developed using only peer-reviewed science, and the report itself was subject to multiple peer reviews, including review by the independent EPA Science Advisory Board.

The Supreme Court's decisions in *Riverside Bayview*, *SWANCC*, and *Rapanos* provide critical context and guidance in determining the appropriate scope of "waters of the United States" covered by the CWA. In the rule, the agencies interpret the scope of "waters of the United States" for the CWA in light of the goals, objectives, and policies of the statute, the Supreme Court case law, the relevant and available science, and the agencies technical expertise and experience.